Essential Oils

Written by Mike Dowling

TOP THAT!

Copyright © 2003 Top That! Publishing plc,
Top That! USA, 27023 McBean Parkway, #408 Valencia, CA 91355
Top That! is a Registered Trademark of Top That! Publishing plc
All rights reserved
www.topthatpublishing.com

contents

Sensory smells	4	
The essentials	6	
Using essential oils	8	
Oil burners	10	
Lamp rings	12	
Personal diffusers	14	
Carrier oils	16	
Macerated oils	18	
The essential oils	20	
Blending oils	22	
Blending oils as perfumes	24	
Bathing beauties	26	
Oils used for candles	28	
Bad hair day?	29	
Scenting clothes and linens	32	
Apricot kernel	34	
Avocado	36	
Basil	38	
Bay	40	
Black pepper	42	
Borage	44	
Chamomile	46	
Cedarwood	48	
Citronella	50	
Clary sage	52	
Clove bud	54	
Cypress and Eucalyptus	56	

Evening primose	58
Fennel	60
Frankincense	62
Geranium	64
Ginger	66
Grapefruit	68
Grapeseed and Jasmine	70
Jojoba	72
Juniper	74
Lavender	76
Lemon	78
Lemongrass	80
Lime	82
Mandarin	84
Marjoram	86
Myrrh	88
Neroli	90
Niaouli	92
Orange	94
Palmarosa	96
Patchouli	98
Peach kernel	100
Peppermint	102
Petitgrain	104
Rosemary	106
Rose otto	108
Rosewood	110

Sandalwood	112
Spearmint	114
Sweet almond	116
Tangerine	118
Tea tree	120
Thyme	122
Vetivert	124
Ylang ylang	126
Closing	128

smells

Our sense of smell, medically known as "olfaction," is probably one of our most underrated senses and we take it so much for granted. Although not as well equipped as other animals, humans have the ability to learn, and accurately remember, many thousands of different scents. Better still, we can improve our sense with practice, as it is the only human sense that actually increases its ability and grows with use.

Culturally, we place great importance upon smell: we give flowers and perfumes to those we love and are constantly bombarded with advertising encouraging us to buy products to mask less pleasant aromas.

This box set is designed to provide an introductory insight into the wonderful world of essential oils and the ways in which they can be safely and enjoyably used.

the essentials

an introduction

"Essential oils" is an interesting name as these substances are neither "essential" nor "oils." They do not seem to be vital to the plants from which they come and they are not oily. So what are they? They are actually very complex mixtures of hundreds of different chemicals called hydrocarbons.

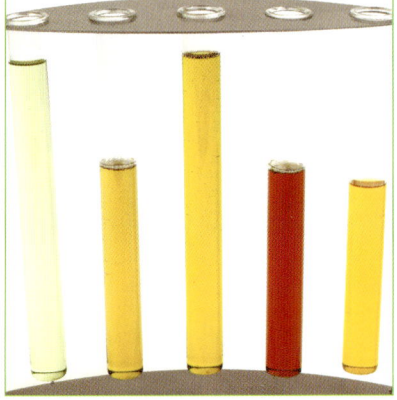

The chemicals are made up of tiny pieces of matter called molecules and it is the way in which these join together, and the shapes they make, that give each substance its unique fragrance and individual properties. It sounds complicated, and indeed it is, but that does not stop us enjoying the scents of these substances and making use of their special therapeutic properties.

are they?

Essential oils are found in tiny amounts in all aromatic plants. The extraction process removes them and puts a great deal in a small bottle. It is important to remember that these are very powerful substances and only tiny amounts should be used. Just consider the delicious aroma of a rose. It takes thirty individual roses to make one drop of rose oil,

and while you might use half a drop as a perfume, you would look very strange with a bunch of flowers behind your ear!

Peppermint oil is renowned for combating indigestion but one drop of oil would flavor a whole box of extra strong mints!

using
essential oils

There are many enjoyable ways of safely using essential oils and we will explore some of them in the following pages. Remember, essential oils you buy in bottles are very strong and only tiny amounts need to be used at any one time.

Also, all essential oils are extremely volatile which means they burn very easily and they must be used with extra care, especially when they are vaporized for fragrancing rooms. You can experiment with different mixes and we will have a look at how to blend various oils together to make massage oils, hair care products, perfumes and bath additives. Learn how to scent your own candles and clothes and use them for creating an atmosphere that could help your own health and well being.

oil burners

the different types

There are a wide variety of burners commercially available and they are typically made from glass, metal, or ceramic materials. They consist of a holder for a small candle, or tea light, over which sits a container or tray to take water and essential oils. It is very important that water is used in the container to prevent the oils from heating too rapidly.

A few drops of one, or a mixture of essential oils are then added to the water. Most will float on the surface although a few will sink to the bottom.

Light the candle underneath and, as the water heats, the oils are gently warmed and evaporate into the room.

As long as they are safely placed, these burners can be a really useful method of dispersing oils. They can be used in sick rooms to help with breathing and colds. Try oils like marjoram, sandalwood, or tea tree.

To freshen a room and lighten the air, try using the enclosed lemon oil. If romance is the order of the day, why not try the rose oil. Although not essential oils, these fragrant oils have been specifically designed just for use with the oil burner included.

& electric diffusers

Lamp rings are usually small, circular, ceramic or metal rings that are like a hollow trough, and sit on top of an upward-pointing light bulb.

A few drops of essential oil can be placed in the hollow and the ring sits on top of the light bulb. As the light warms up the oils evaporate into the room. They are quite effective but do make sure the light cannot be knocked and do not use a bulb stronger that 60 watts. It is quite surprising how hot these rings can get, so allow them to cool properly before removing them. They are not advisable for children's rooms.

There are several electric diffusers that are commercially available though they can be quite expensive and are not very pretty. They work either by containing an electric heating element that warms a container for essential oils, or by passing air from a fan through an absorbent pad onto which oils have been placed.

They are most effective for fragrancing larger rooms and will run safely for long periods of time.

personal
diffusers

Why not make your own diffuser? All you need is a small can with some holes in it. Pop inside a pad of lint or absorbent cotton onto which you can place the essential oils of your choice. You can keep these in your purse or desk and use them whenever you like. Try ginger or peppermint if you suffer from travel sickness or neroli or petitgrain if you know you are going to be in a stressful situation.

Keep one handy with citronella or lemongrass to ward off unwanted insects. Peppermint placed strategically will stop mice visiting!

You can use this same method if you do not have a burner or other diffuser. Just place your tin on top of a radiator and use it to fragrance the room.

oils

Essential oils are very strong and if you want to use them for massage or for the skin they must be diluted. Unlike essential oils, carrier oils do not evaporate when they are heated and so they are sometimes called "fixed" oils. There is a wide choice available and those covered in this book include apricot kernel, avocado, evening primrose, grapeseed, peach kernel and sweet almond. Jojoba is really a liquid wax but can be included for our purposes.

While carrier oils vary greatly in price do not be tempted to compromise. Always try to get "cold pressed" oils, sometimes called "extra virgin," from a reputable supplier.

Which oil you decide to use is really down to personal preference. Some have a distinct fragrance of their own while others are quite bland. Carrier oils tend not to last as long as essential oils once they have been opened. About three months is an average, after which they go rancid. This is a process called "oxidation" where the oil combines with air and develops a rather unpleasant smell (just like cooking oil that has been left too long). Adding ten per cent of wheatgerm oil will make your mixtures last twice as long.

You can usually buy small quantities of carrier oils so that you do not waste them. Keep your bottles as full as possible to eliminate air and keep them in a cool dark place.

Oils

These are sometimes called "infused" oils and tend to be made commercially when the amount of essential oil in a plant is very small and expensive to extract. Calendula or marigold oil is probably the best known but others include St. John's wort, carrot, and melissa or lemon balm. They are made by soaking the plant material in a carrier oil and leaving it to stand, often in a warm place or on a window sill. The essential oils are dissolved into the carrier oil and impart their fragrance. After some time, the oil is strained to remove the exhausted plant material and the process repeated until the desired strength is obtained.

If you have large amounts of herbs in your garden you can try this method yourself. Almond or sunflower oil are both worth using, as neither of these smell strongly themselves. Many gardens have lavender, lemon balm, or rosemary bushes, all of which work really well, and you can make good use of the bits you prune. You can always use the plant remnants on the compost heap afterwards.

the essential oils

An essential oil is described as an aromatic, volatile substance extracted from a single botanical source by distillation or expression.

This means that they have a distinctive and usually fragrant smell, and evaporate easily and rapidly into the air when warmed, enabling us to detect them.

A pure essential oil is obtained from one type of plant either by distillation, which involves heating the plant material with steam or hot water and separating the resulting vapor, or by expression, where plant material is crushed to squeeze out the "oil."

It is the essential oils that give plants their individual aroma or spices their "flavor." Pure oils are very expensive as plants only contain minute amounts. They dissolve only in alcohol or carrier oils and while they do not dissolve in water, they will impart their fragrance to it. They are very precious substances and provide us with the most wonderful natural pharmacy.

It is important to find a reputable supplier who will only provide the best-quality oils that will do what you believe they can and last for the longest time.

oils

They should be supplied in dropper bottles with tamper-evident tops. Once you have purchased your oils you must keep them in dark, airtight bottles in a cool place.

We will look at a variety of essential oils with many properties, and prices varying from very reasonable to extremely expensive, but they are all amazing substances.

WARNING: Essential oils should NEVER be taken internally.

blending oils

Blending oils is something of an art but we all have to start somewhere. It is vital that essential oils are diluted before use on the skin as a massage oil. This will usually be done in a carrier oil although creams and shampoos can be used as well.

The maximum concentration of essential oils for adults should not exceed two per cent and for children under fourteen, one per cent. This sounds complicated but is quite simple to work out. The size of a drop from an essential oil bottle is remarkably uniform which is handy. One hundred drops of oil equals one teaspoon.

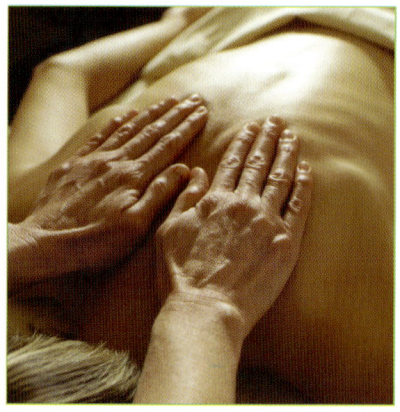

So, for a one per cent dilution you would use one drop of essential oil per teaspoon of carrier and for a two per cent dilution, two drops. A single teaspoon is enough for a face massage and a full body massage would take about five teaspoonfuls, so you just add drops of essential oils accordingly.

oils

In perfumery, oils are classified as top, middle, or base notes, according to the rate at which they evaporate and how strong they are when blended. This becomes quite complex but the following will simplify it.

The citrus oils are usually "top notes," the woody oils are "base notes," and herbaceous plants are "middle notes." To obtain a balanced blend you should try and use oils from different sections together. For example, use one top and another middle, or one top and a base, or one from each. As a very rough guide use them in the ratio of 1:2:3—that is, three drops of a top note to one drop of a base or two of a middle note.

The best way is to experiment. Try small quantities to start with and make sure you make a note of how many drops of each oil you have used. Don't forget, start gently. You can always add more oil but you can't take it away. Also, it is advisable not to use more than three essential oils together or your blend can become nondescript and difficult to recreate.

blending oils

as perfumes

For perfumes the rules are not really different from before. However, it is important to know about "fixing." Because essential oils evaporate quickly, especially the top notes, you have to hold them back or "fix" them with a base note to make the fragrance last for a longer time.

Most of the woody oils, like sandalwood, cedarwood, vetivert, or patchouli can be used and just one drop in a mixture will help you obtain a scent that lingers.

Let us suppose you want a perfume that smells of orange. You might use ten drops in the creation of your mixture but you could include just one drop of sandalwood to fix it.

You can make your perfume using a carrier oil as before but commercial perfumes are made using pure alcohol and water. The benefit of using alcohol is that it is less greasy and water can be added. For home use you can use vodka, as it doesn't really smell of anything itself. Once you have mixed your blend you can then add water to dilute it and apply it as you would an ordinary perfume. The longer a perfume lasts, the more expensive it is so, who knows, you could experiment and create a new and valuable fragrance by yourself!

beauties

This is a really good way of using essential oils as not only do you benefit from a long, hot soak, but the oils have a chance to give you their benefits as well.

Many books tell you to add essential oils to your bath but care is needed when you do. You should never add neat oils to your bathtub, especially as they have a nasty habit of corroding plastic tubs.

Once you have decided which oils you would like to use, mix them first with a little shampoo, liquid soap, or even full fat milk. You can purchase unfragranced bath oil from suppliers and add your oils to that instead. This helps the oils to mix with the water, otherwise they tend to sit on the surface and you can get a drop of oil in some very sensitive places! You can use just one oil or continue your blending skills and be adventurous.

oils used

for candles

Essential oils blend very well with waxes and lots of people make their own candles. Commercially, between three per cent and seven per cent of essential oils are added while the wax is molten and you can try this if making your own. If you do not have the facilities you can take existing unfragranced candles and warm them until soft in a bowl of hot water. When soft, remove them and

place some drops of essential oil on the wax. You will find that the oils absorb quite well. You can also add drops of oil to the melted wax of a burning unscented candle but do be careful as essential oils are extremely flammable. It is better to blow out the candle, add the essential oils and then carefully re-light it.

hair day?

Shampoo bases are very difficult to make for yourself but are fairly easy to obtain from a good supplier. You need to get an unfragranced mix so that it doesn't affect the addition of essential oils. You should use the same percentage of essential oils as for massage oils, which is two per cent.

Rosemary is a wonderful oil to give shine and luster to hair and is worth adding to almost any shampoo mix as it helps with dandruff, dryness, itching, and even unwanted visitors.

Lemongrass and rosemary together will see off head lice. Wash the hair with the mixture and try to leave it on for about ten minutes before rinsing. If that doesn't do the trick, try tea tree next time.

hair day?

For greasy hair, bergamot, cypress, geranium, sandalwood, lemon, or ylang ylang could be added. Chamomile brings a real brightness to blonde or dry hair. Jojoba is good for dryness and dandruff and really helps to revitalize the scalp, roots, and body of the hair.

For partial hair loss, try a mixture of rosemary, cedarwood, and lavender with some jojoba. Again, leave the mixture on for about ten minutes before rinsing and, as they say, watch this space!

With all the time and energy that people put into their hair and the treatments they subject it to, it is hardly surprising that hair becomes damaged. Jojoba in particular is useful as a rescue treatment. It coats

the hair and helps the scalp return to producing normal sebum, which keeps the hair in good condition. The addition of some rosemary, cypress, or black pepper will help stimulate the blood supply to the hair follicles, prevent irritation, and encourage hair growth.

scenting
clothes and linens

We are constantly encouraged to have our clothes smelling of spring meadows and mountain freshness, but why not save money and do it yourself?

We have already discussed personal diffusers and these can easily be placed in clothes drawers or closets to infuse laundry with the fragrance of your own choosing. Small ceramic amphoras can be purchased which are made of absorbent, unglazed porcelain.

These soak up essential oils and release them slowly into the air around clothes.

You can add essential oils to distilled water and put the mixture into a spray bottle. You can then spray your clothes, bed linen, furniture, or whatever you like to give them your favorite aroma. You can even add oils to your steam iron and add fragrance to yourself, your clothes, and the room all at once. A word of caution, however: essential oils are not fond of synthetic materials so, if in doubt, spray a test patch where it doesn't show before spraying everything.

You can also add essential oils to your washing machine to give homemade "spring freshness" to your whole wash!

Prunus Armeniaca

A lovely, light, pale yellow oil which has a slight smell of marzipan. It is very easily absorbed into the surface of the skin. It contains vitamins A and C and is suitable for all types of skin, especially prematurely aged, inflamed, dry, and sensitive. It can help relieve itching and makes a lovely base for a face or body massage. Good quality oil is, however, very expensive.

avocado

Persea Americana

This oil is extracted from the flesh of the fruit. It is thick and green in color but the oil goes cloudy when cold. It does not keep for very long but is very rich and probably best used when mixed with another carrier oil such as sweet almond.

It is rich in vitamins and potassium and can relieve the itching of psoriasis and eczema. It is softening and soothing and makes a wonderful hand cream.

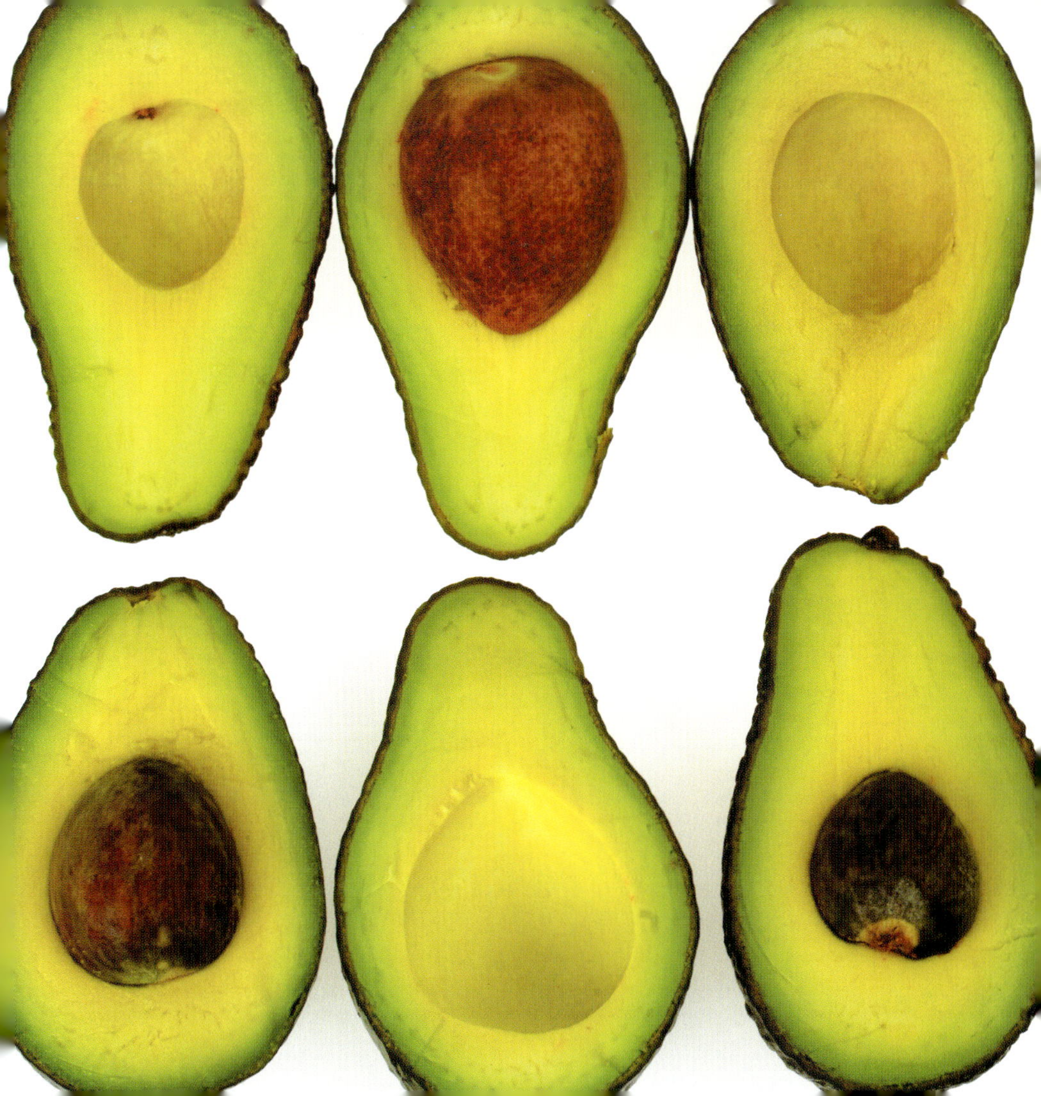

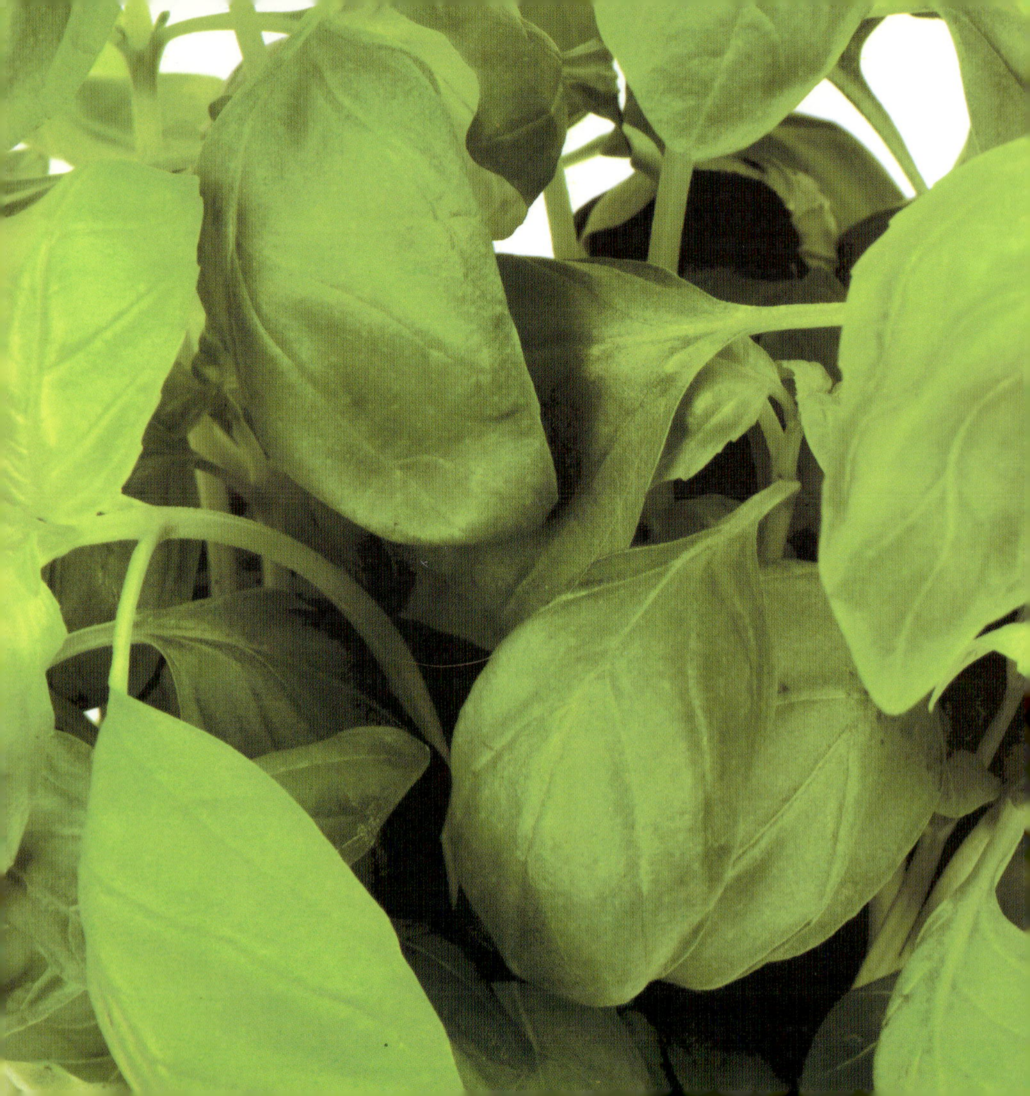

Ocimum basilicum

This is a pale yellow oil with a distinct smell of aniseed. It is a good stimulant for the nervous system, particularly for the brain. It can help with poor memory and indecision. You can use it for indigestion, and insects do not like it so it works as a repellent. It should be avoided during pregnancy.

WARNING: Basil oil can contain a chemical which is very poisonous.

bay

Laurus Nobilis

This is a very spicy, medicinal-smelling oil. It is good for the respiratory system and is often used for coughs and colds. It can be used to help aching muscles and rheumatism. However, the main use has been in cosmetic preparations including soaps and aftershave, although it is also used in processed foods and drinks.

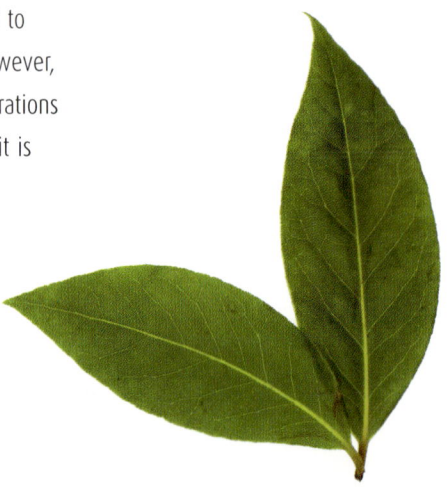

WARNING: It should be avoided during pregnancy and can cause skin irritation in some people.

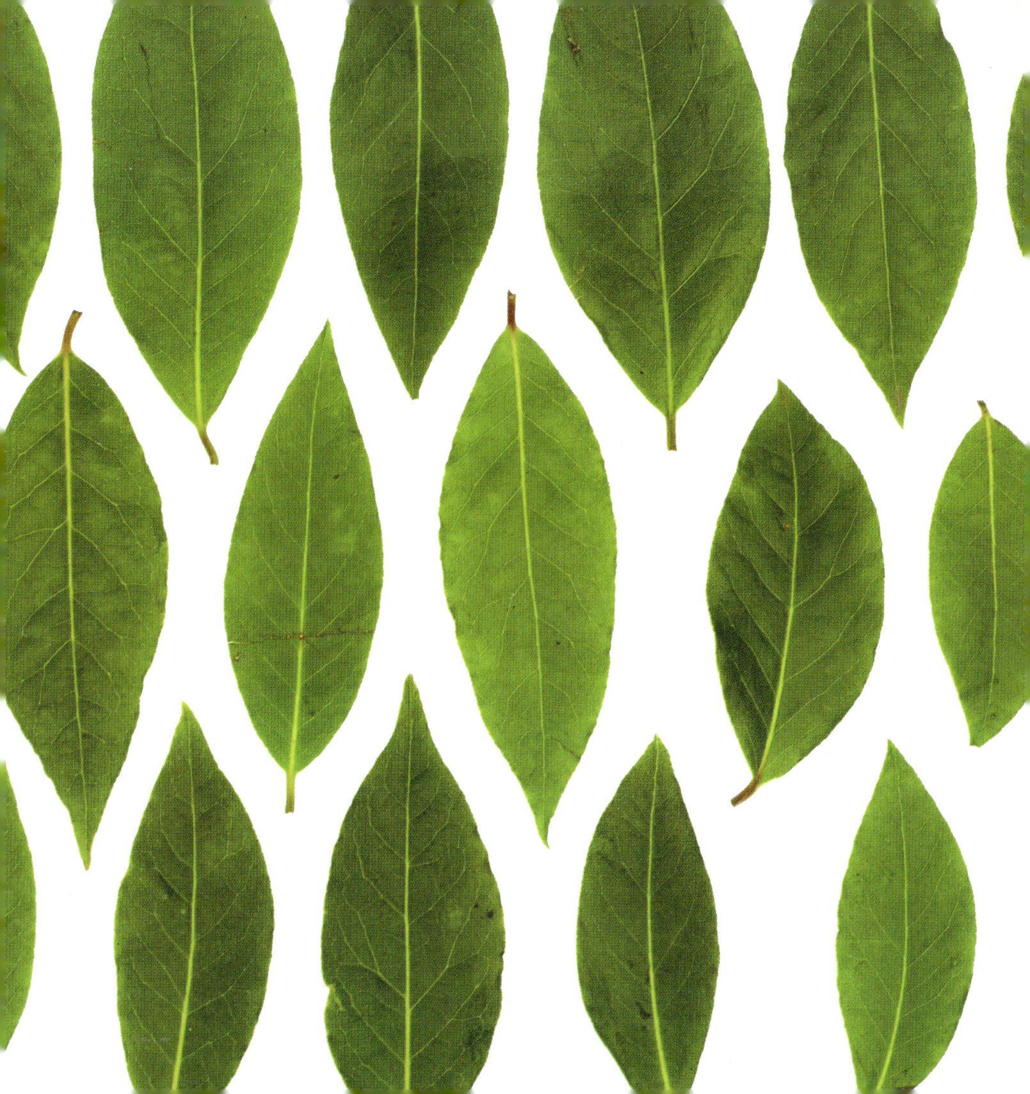

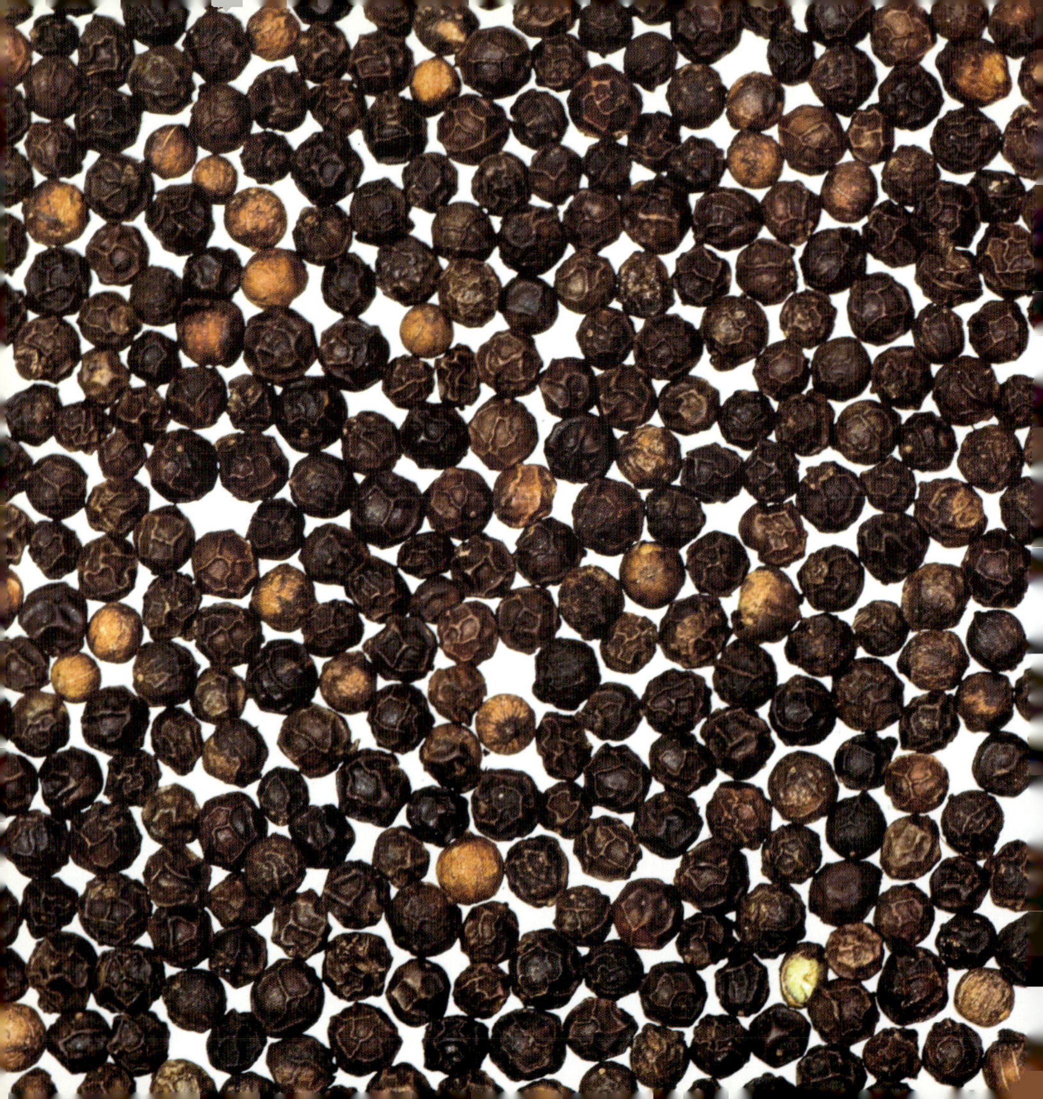

Piper Nigrum

This is a colorless or very pale yellow oil which smells hot and peppery as you might expect. It is wonderful for muscular aches and rheumatism and can help with the restoration of muscle tone after long-term injury. Chilblain sufferers may well find one drop of oil in a footbath really helpful. The oil, like the berries it comes from, aids digestion and stimulates the appetite. It blends well with frankincense, sandalwood, lavender, and rosemary.

Borago Officinalis

This colorless oil is obtained from the seeds of the beautiful borage plant, also known as starflower because of the shape of the flowers, and bee bread because of their attraction to bees. The oil contains a very high level of GLA (Gamma Linoleic Acid) and is useful in disorders where nerves have been damaged. It is very good for skin disorders including eczema and psoriasis and as an anti-inflammatory for rheumatism.

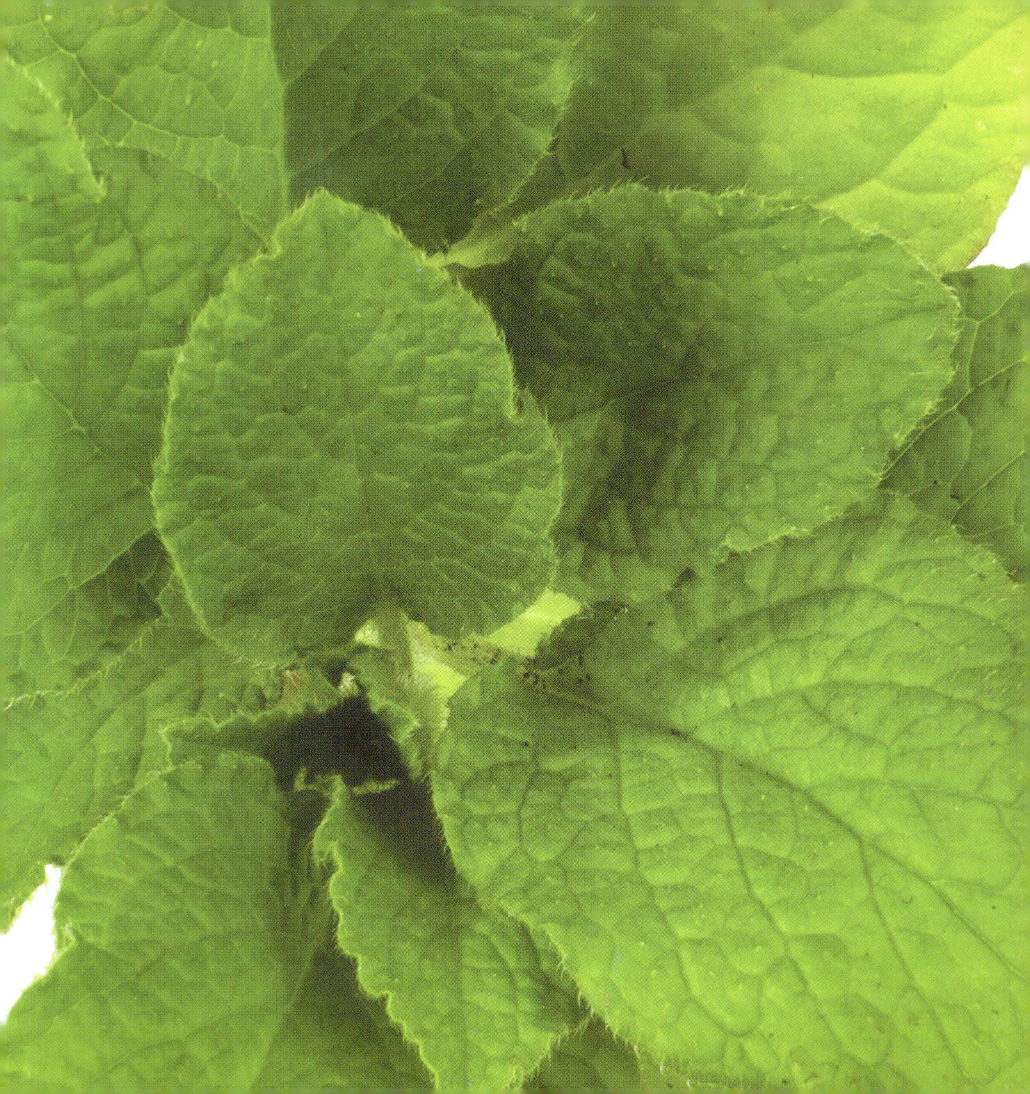

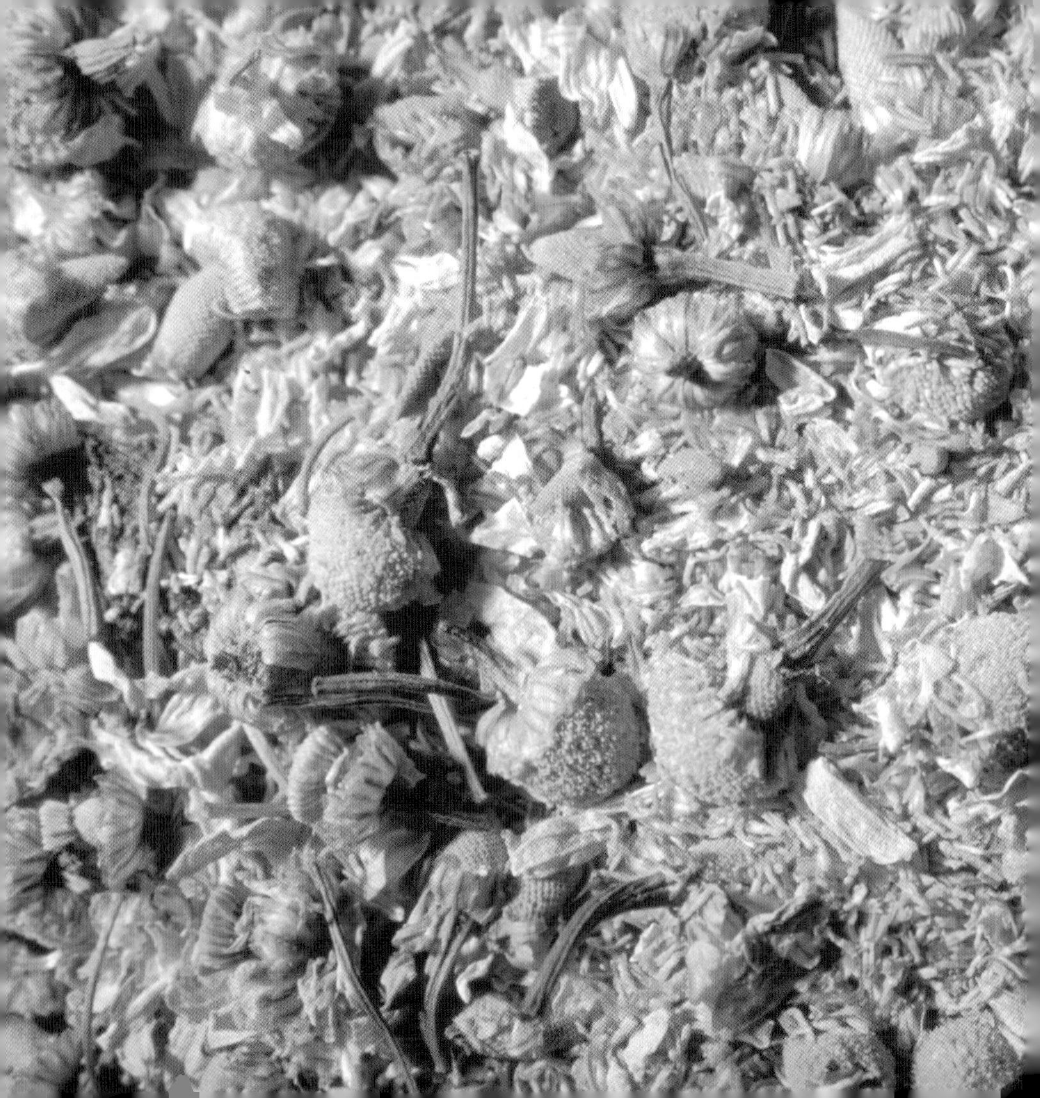

Anthemis Nobilis

This is a very pale blue oil that turns yellow as it ages. It has a herbaceous and fruity aroma and is excellent for children's problems including teething and colic. It has very good anti-inflammatory properties for bites and stings, and aches and pains. It is particularly good for PMS and period pains; try mixing some with clary sage in a massage oil and putting some on the abdomen and lower back. It is a calming oil and good for angry people.

cedarwood

Cedrus Atlantica

A lovely yellow oil with a soft, sweet and woody aroma reminiscent of pencils. It has particular use in genital and urinary problems including cystitis. Rats and insects do not like it. Skin loves it and it is wonderful for relieving itching, especially from bites, stings, and chickenpox. Add a little to your shampoo if you suffer from dandruff, and if scattered thoughts are your downfall, try some on your diffuser to concentrate the mind. It blends well with bergamot, rose, neroli, and rosemary.

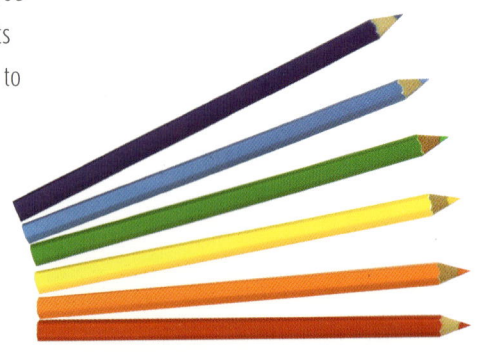

WARNING: Avoid cedarwood oil if you are pregnant.

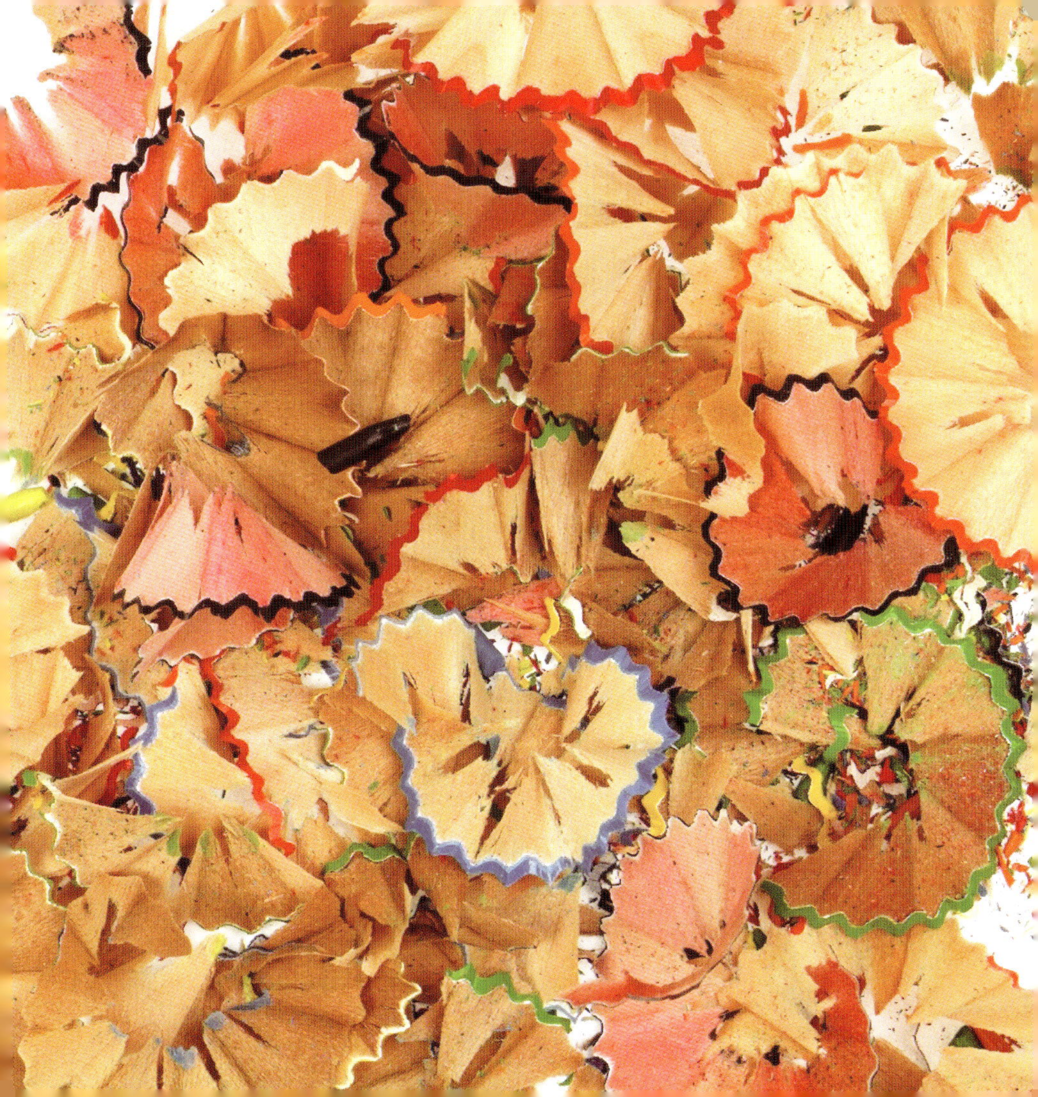

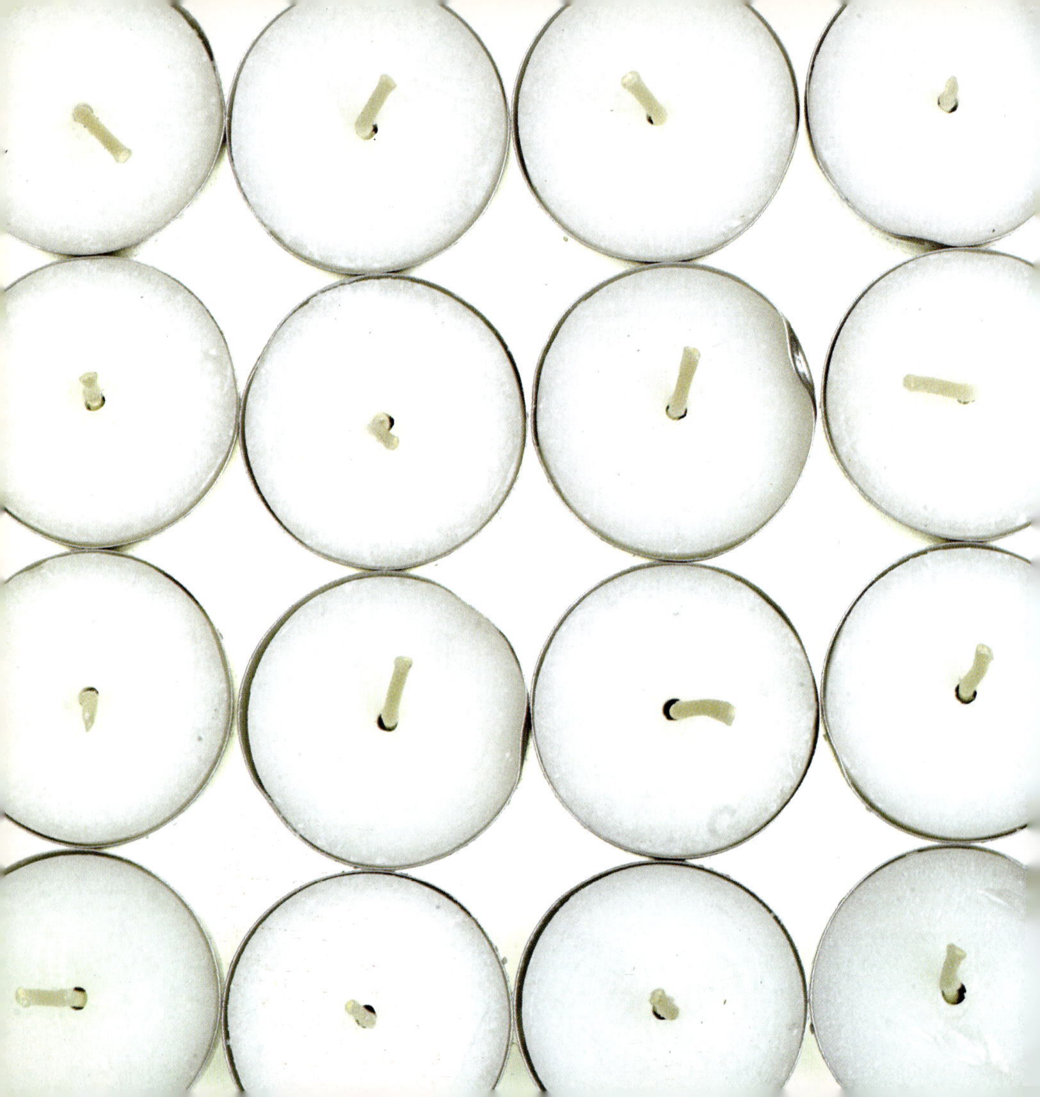

citronella

Cymbopogon Nardus

This yellow oil has a sharp lemony smell and will be familiar to anyone who has bought insect repellents. Insects detest the smell and a bottle should be kept in every traveling bag! You can add a drop to a massage oil or to rose water to keep the bugs at bay and it will also help to rid animals of fleas but do mind their noses—it smells ten times stronger to them. Citronella candles help make summer barbecues bearable and clothes shut in drawers moth-free.

clary sage

Salvia Sclarea

This colorless oil has a smell a little reminiscent of damp paper. It has a tonic effect on the nervous system and makes some people feel very light headed, though it is a good relaxing oil. Helpful in combating the Monday morning blues or that heavy feeling after an illness, it is also useful for PMS and period pains, blending well with Roman chamomile for that purpose. It can also help to reduce high blood pressure and prevent insomnia. It blends quite well but try it with lavender, bergamot, orange, or sandalwood.

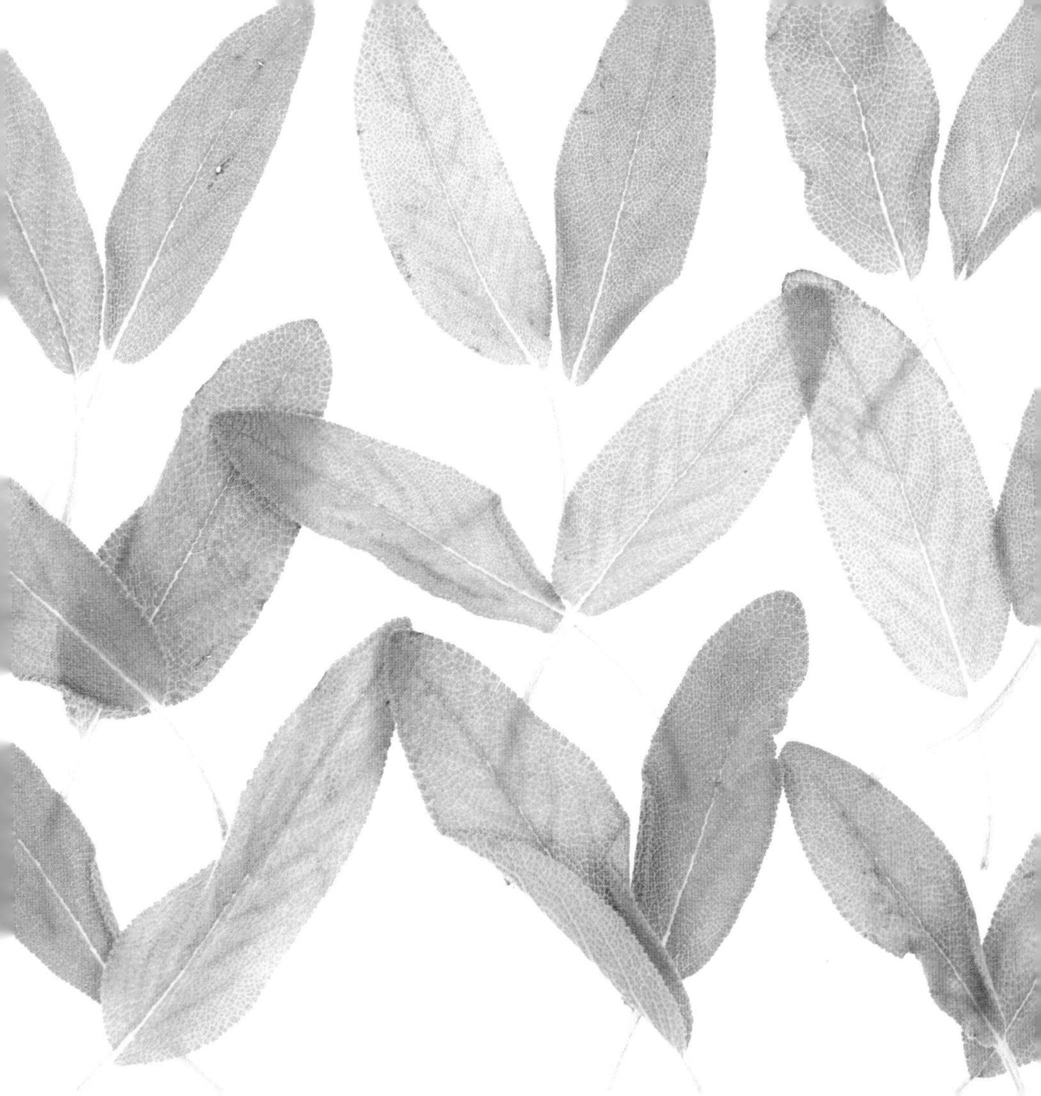

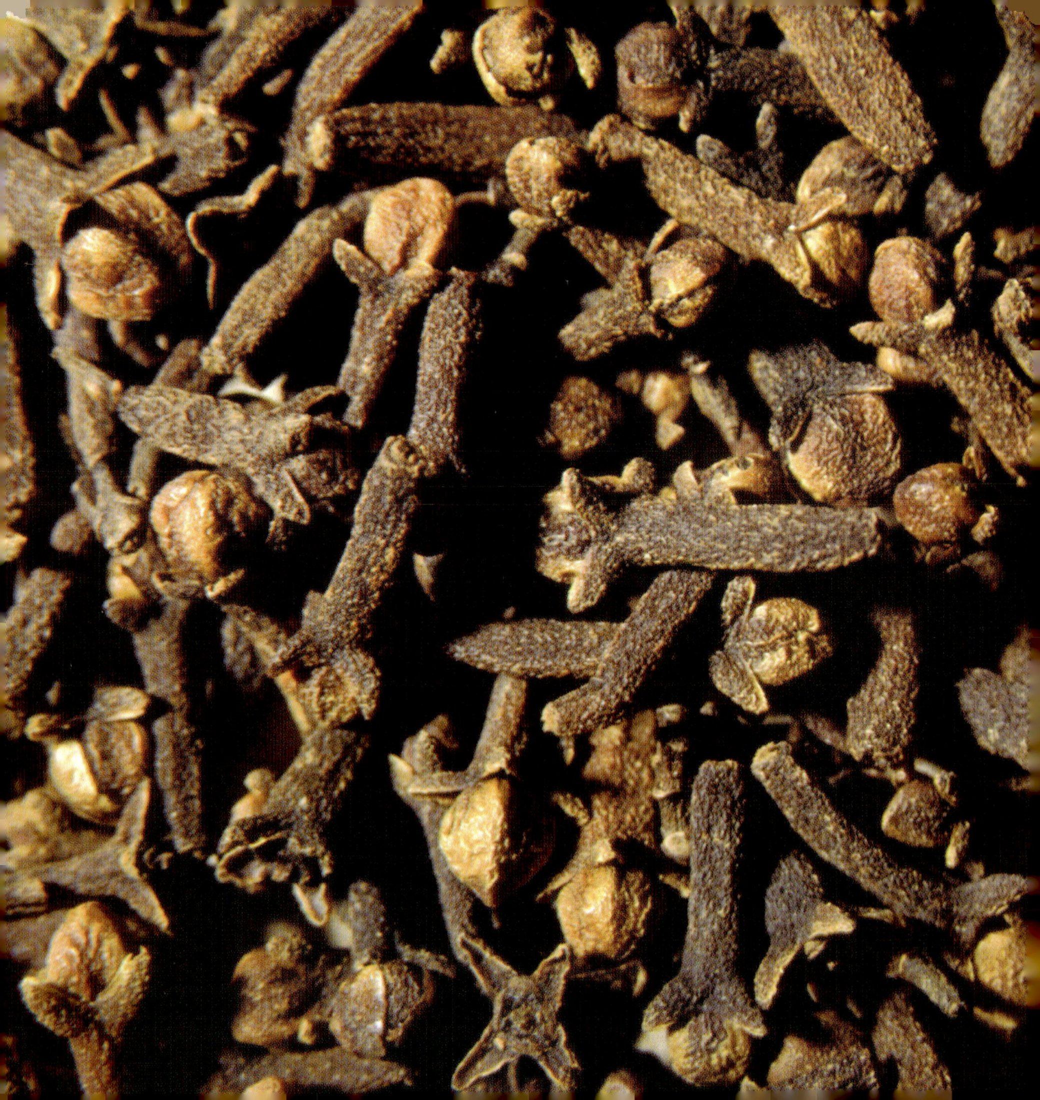

Eugenia Caryophyllata

It is important that only clove bud oil is used, not the leaf or the stem. It has a very characteristic smell and has long been used to repel clothes moths; mosquitoes do not like it either. It is also a classic remedy for toothache and neuralgia as it has strong analgesic properties. It is a powerful antiseptic and can also be used for acne, arthritis, rheumatism, and athlete's foot. Clove oil can cause mucous membrane irritation so be very careful of the nose and eyes and do not apply directly onto the mouth or skin. Its smell makes it difficult to blend but orange or bergamot work well.

Cupressus Sempervirens

This colorless oil has a soft, piney, woody fragrance. It is very useful for all respiratory conditions as it helps to sedate the nerve endings in the tract. Good for coughs, colds, and asthma. It has astringent properties making it valuable in the treatment of varicose veins and hemorrhoids. Often used for menstrual and menopausal disorders, it can also help urinary tract infections. It blends well with clary sage, frankincense, juniper, lavender, or lemongrass.

Eucalyptus Globulus

A colorless oil with a sharp camphoraceous smell. It is a classic remedy for respiratory infections including coughs, colds, throat infections, and congestion. It is very antiseptic. It helps the body to get rid of urea which makes it very valuable in the treatment of muscular aches and pains, rheumatism, gout, and arthritis. It is another oil good for repelling insects. However, it is very strong and is not recommended for use with young children.

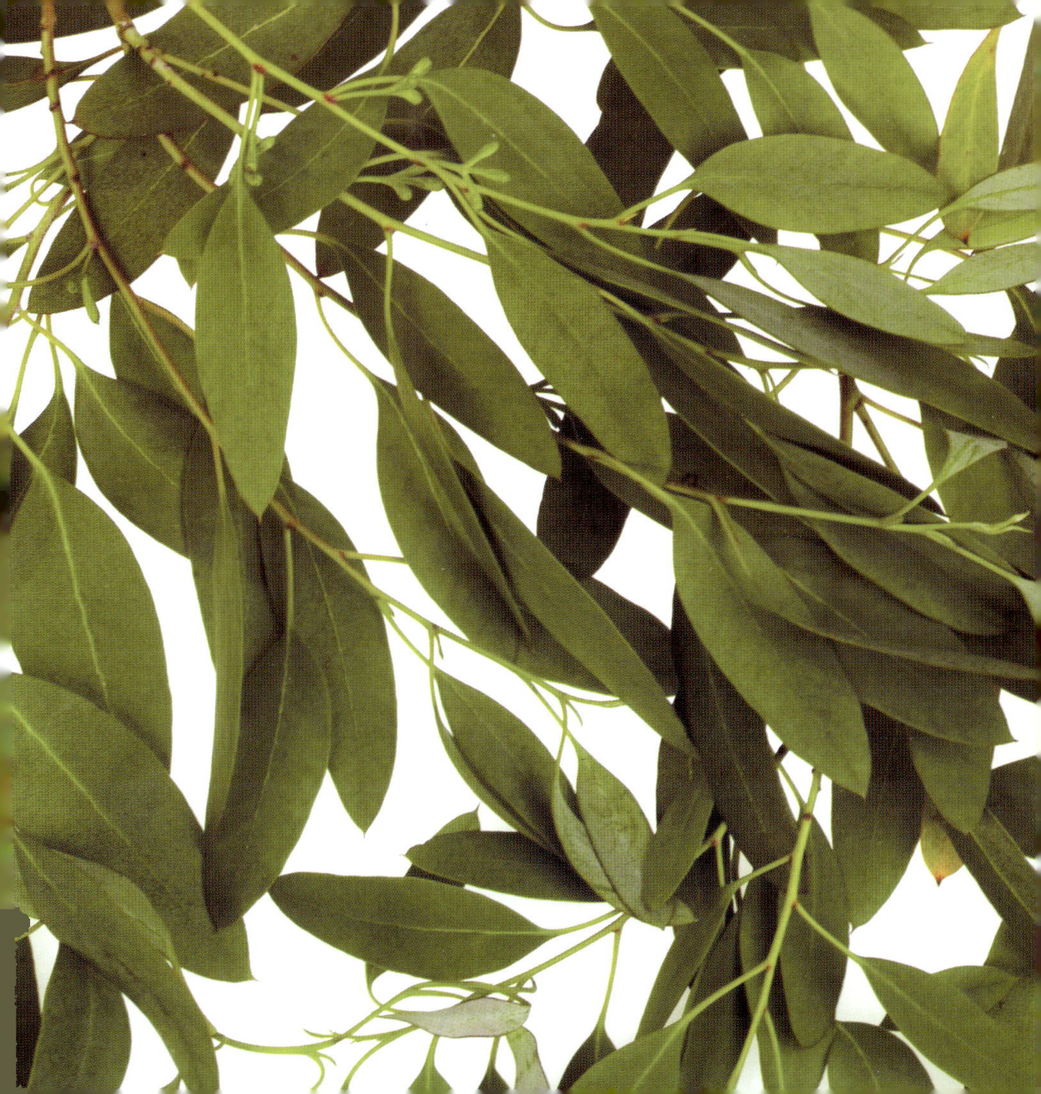

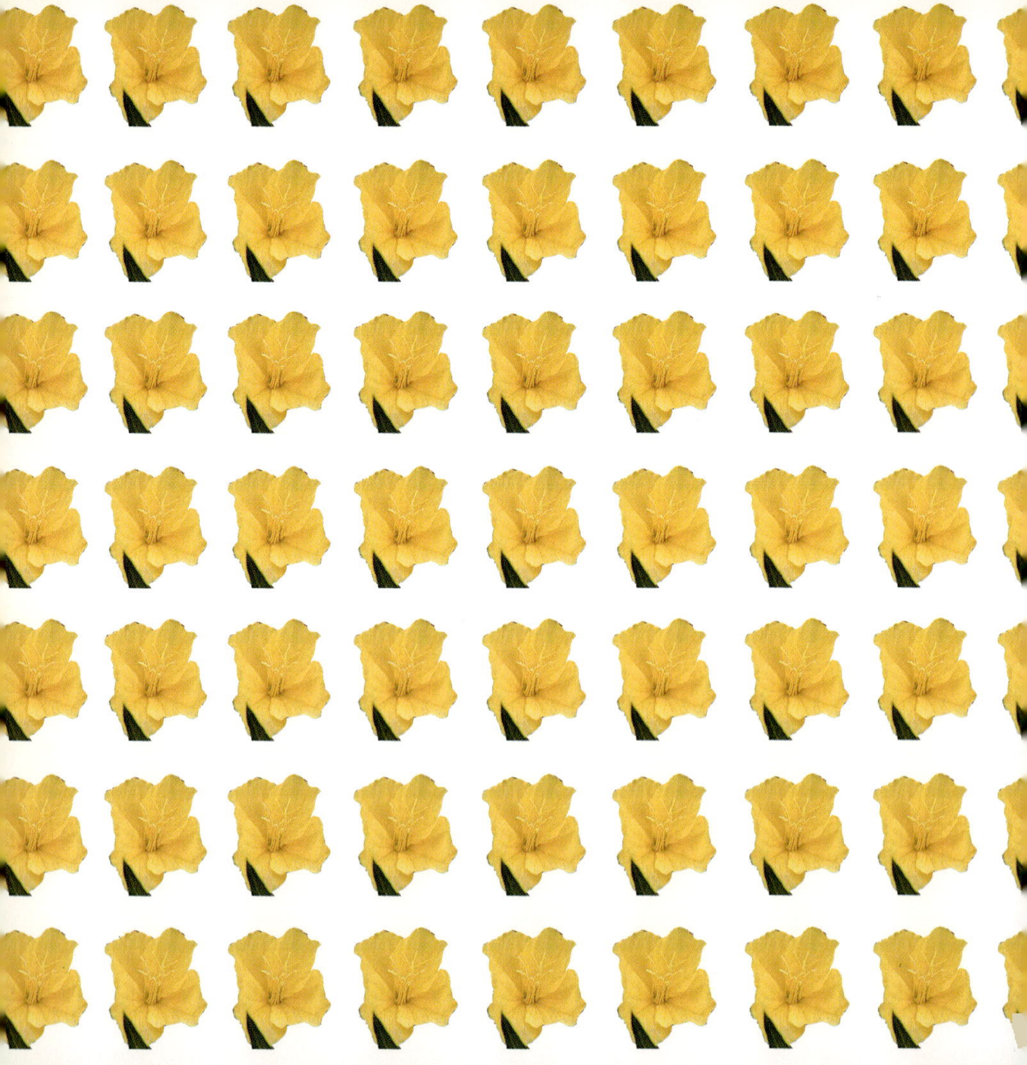

Oenothera Biennis

This pale yellow oil is extracted from the seeds of the plant by expression. It has a high percentage of GLA (Gamma Linoleic Acid) and has become popular in the treatment of PMS and period pains, including associated muscular pains and breast discomfort. It is very effective for dry skin, particularly on the scalp, and is thought to help with premature ageing. It has also become popular in the treatment of arthritis and rheumatism. Whilst rather expensive it makes a good carrier for essential oils and can help accelerate the healing of wounds.

fennel

Foeniculum Vulgare

This is a colorless or pale yellow oil, with an aniseed-like smell. It is a tonic to the digestive system and is used in a proprietary brand for children's colic. It can help with extremes including constipation and diarrhea. Fennel is a diuretic and has traditionally been used in the treatment of obesity. It is "estrogenic" and has uses in the treatment of menopause and pre-menstrual problems. It also stimulates the production of breast milk in nursing mothers but should not be used during pregnancy. Fennel blends quite well with lavender, geranium, and rose.

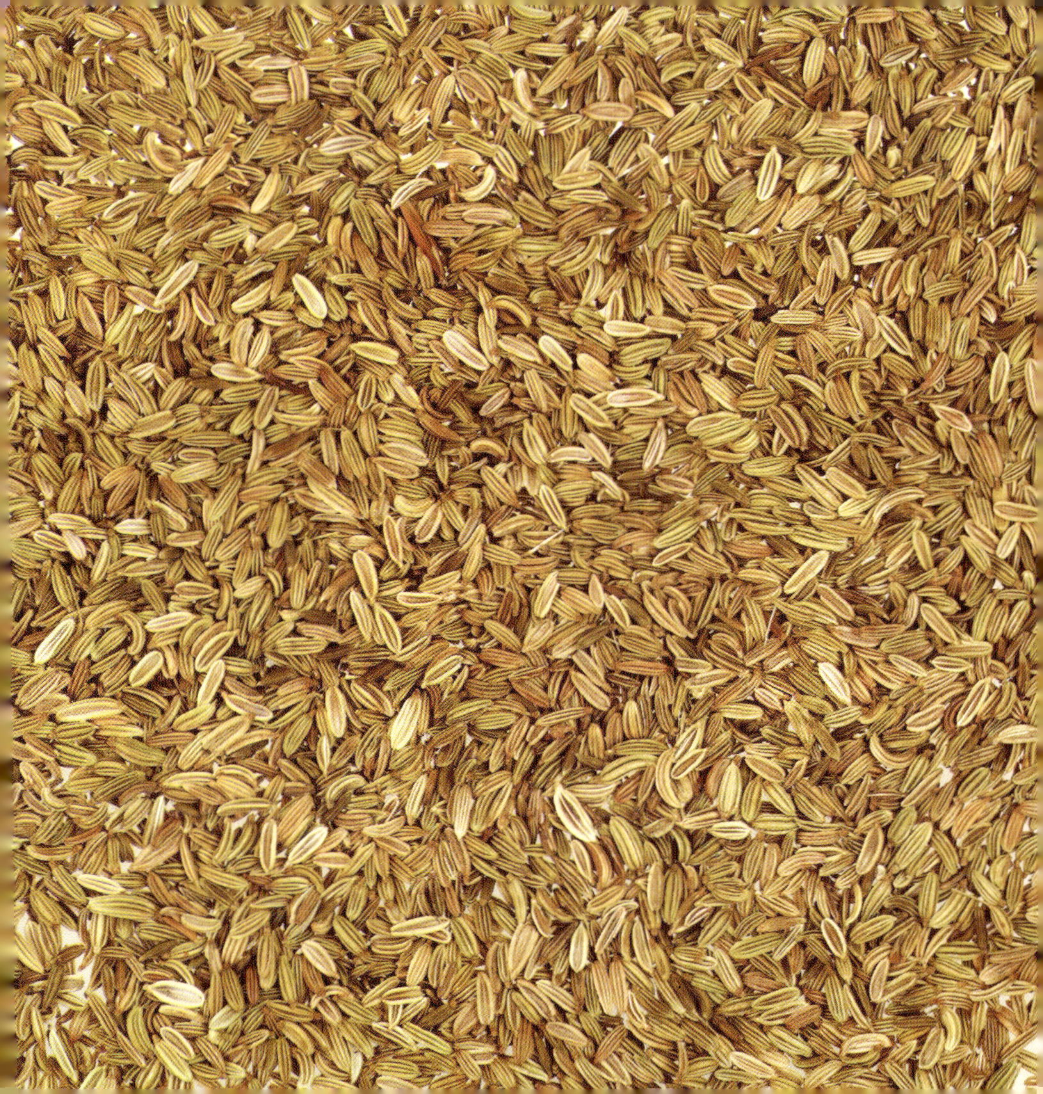

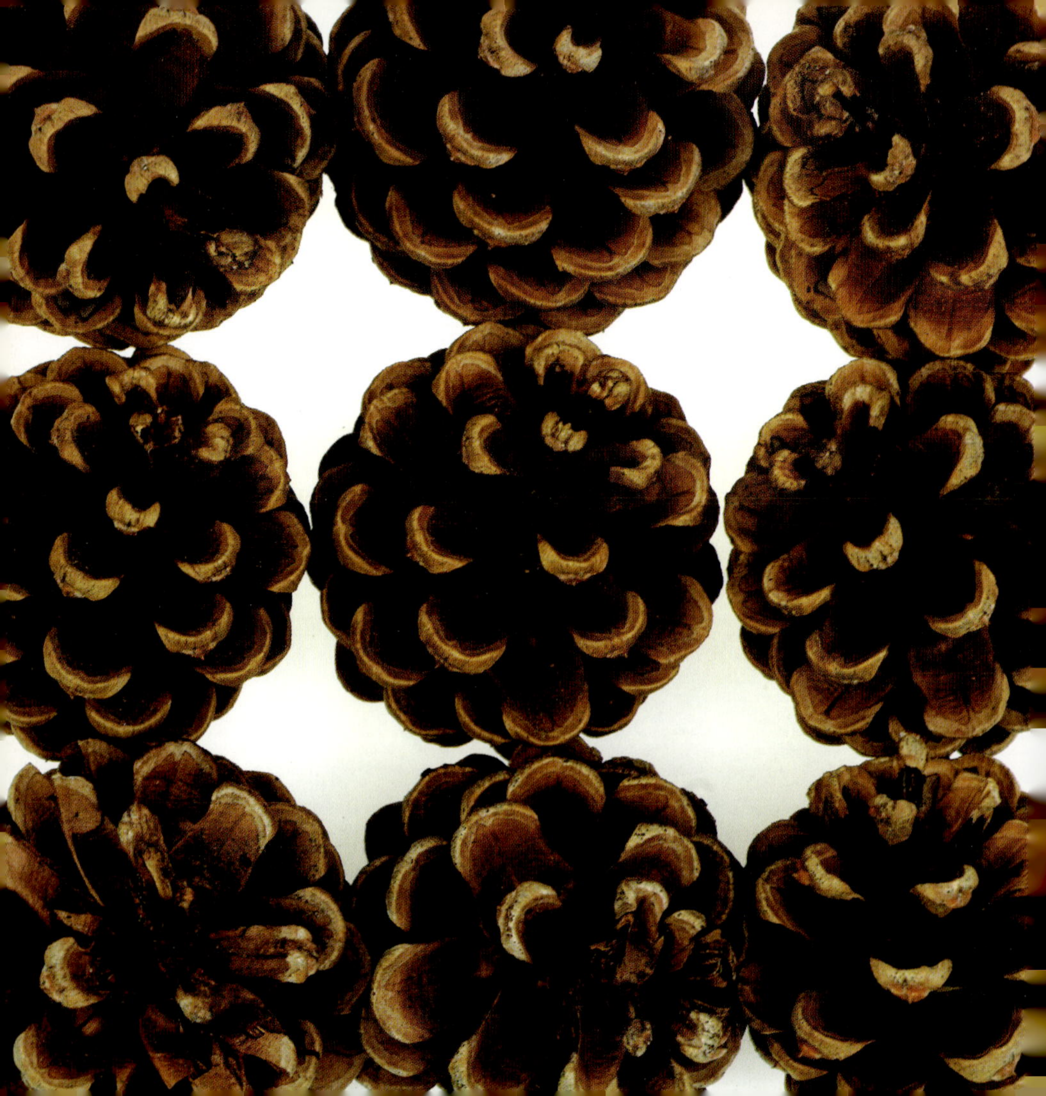

Frankincense

Boswellia Carterii

This oil has a wonderful warm piney smell which feels soft and wraps you up like a blanket. It has astringent properties but helps to heal really stubborn wounds like ulcers and bed sores. It is good for respiratory problems including congestion. Valuable in the treatment of rheumatism and arthritis it seems particularly helpful on more mature users. It is an airborne bactericide and is said to keep away woodworm. When blended with rose oil it is like a "hug in a bottle" and is really comforting. It also blends well with bergamot or grapefruit.

geranium

Pelargonium Odoratissimum

A green-colored oil with a heavy, rosy scent. It is said to be balancing and harmonizing and helps the body to work well as a unit. Like fennel, it contains estrogenic substances which can assist with PMS and menstrual problems. It is a gentle analgesic and antiseptic and is valuable for cuts and burns. Skin problems including broken capillaries, dry skin, acne, and dry eczema will also benefit from this oil's properties. It is another good insect repellent and a useful oil for people who experience mood swings. It blends well with many oils but the citrus oils like grapefruit and orange can help to lift what may be a "heavy" fragrance to some.

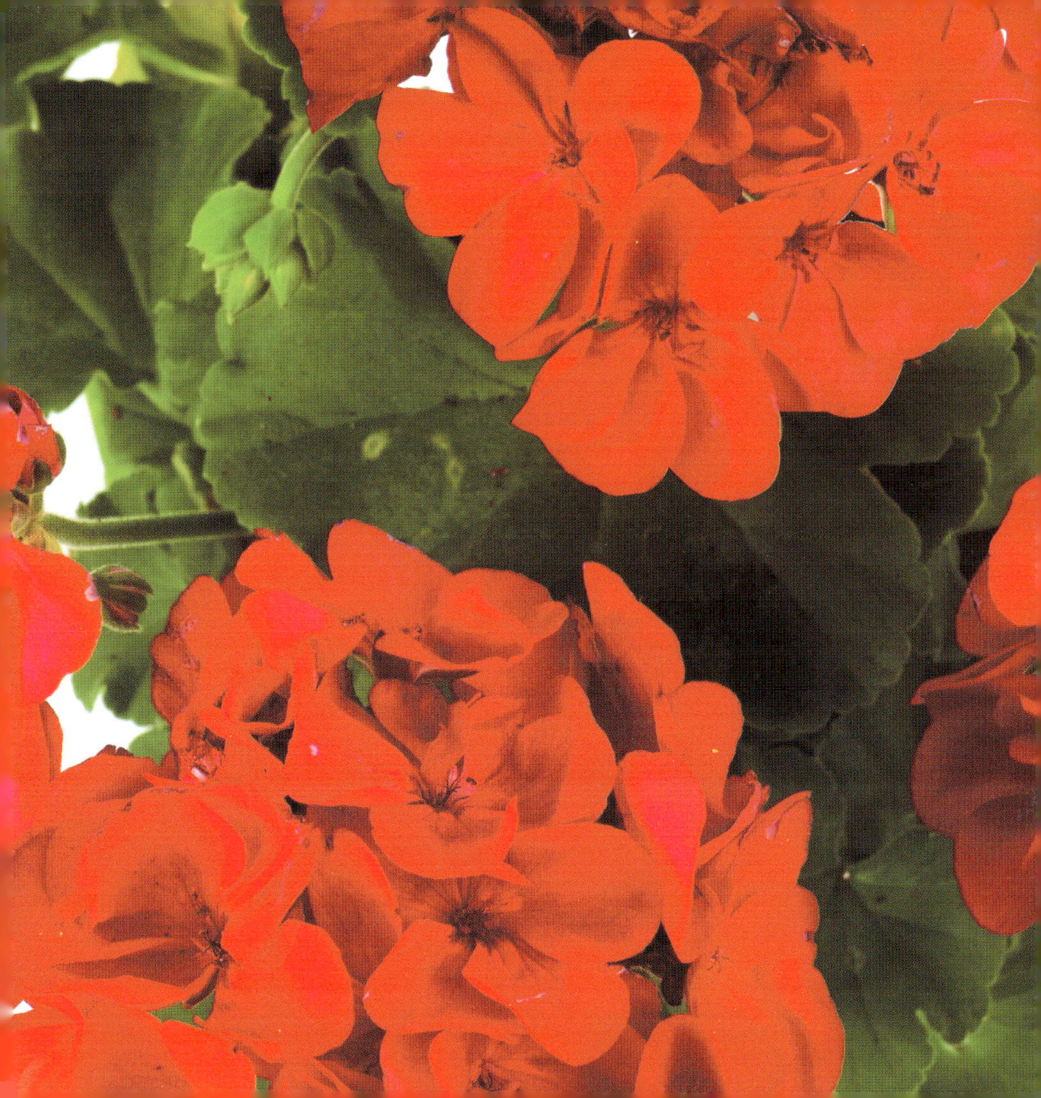

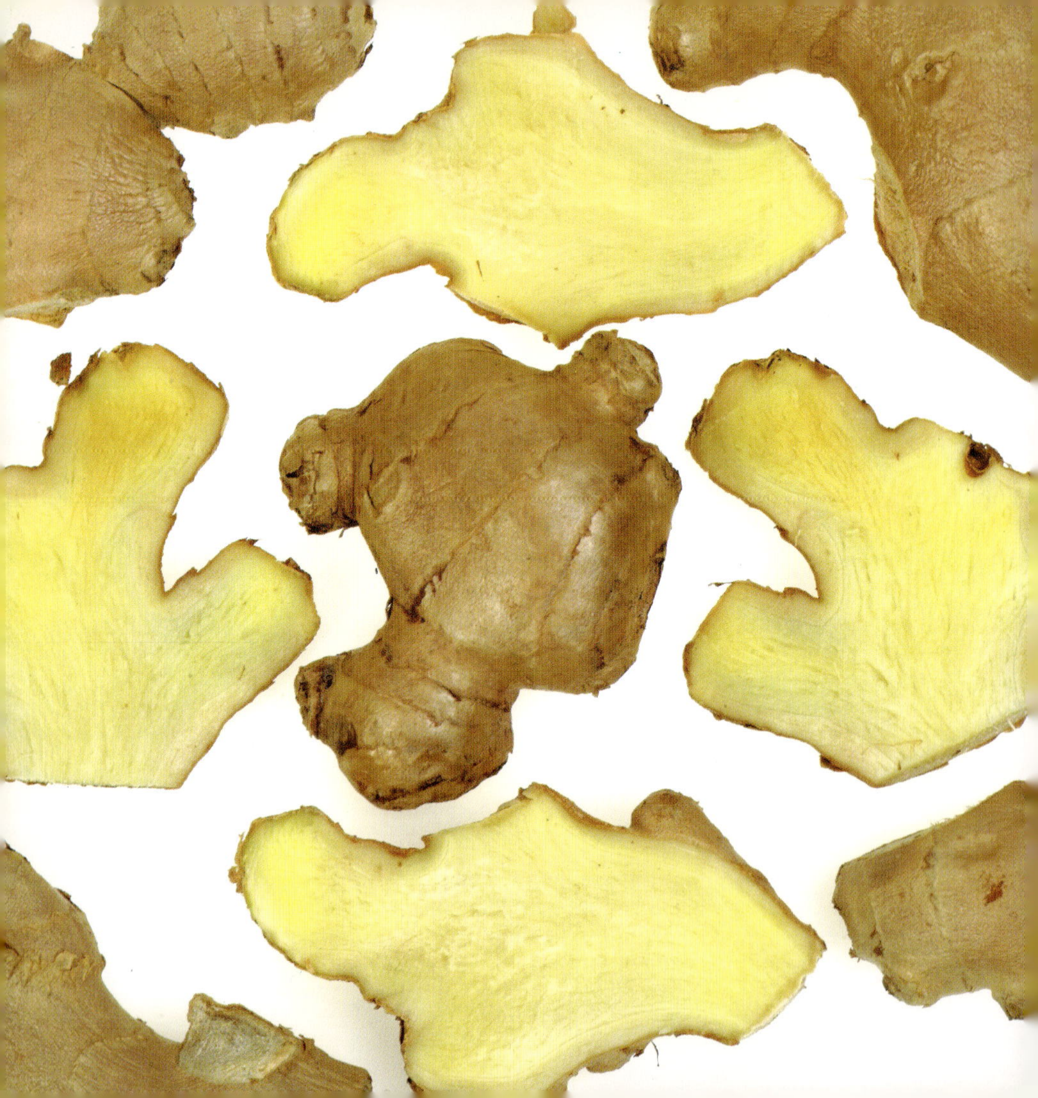

Zingiber Officinalis

Ginger root oil is pale yellow and has a surprisingly fresh but woody smell. Whilst it is probably best known as a digestive aid for diarrhea, indigestion, colic, and loss of appetite, it is wonderful for the treatment of nausea, particularly travel sickness. It is also valuable in cases of arthritis, muscular aches and pains, poor circulation, and rheumatism. Good for catarrh, congestion, coughs, sore throats, and sinusitis. Care should be taken as some people find it increases the skin's sensitivity to ultraviolet light.

grapefruit

Citrus Paradisi

A pale yellow oil extracted from the peel of the grapefruit by expression. It has a wonderfully clean and sharp aroma with a lovely citrus tang. The cleanliness of the smell reflects its function, as it is a good "cleanser," particularly of the digestive system where it works as a liver and blood tonic and so helps to rid the body of toxic substances. It can also help clear the mind and assist with decision making and planning. It is good for all skin types, particularly for oily skin and acne. It is an excellent airborne antiseptic, so is another one for your diffuser. When blending, this can be a very good addition as it lightens and brightens heavier mixes. If you are not sure where it has come from, be careful how you use it in sunlight. Unfortunately, grapefruit oil only keeps for about six months.

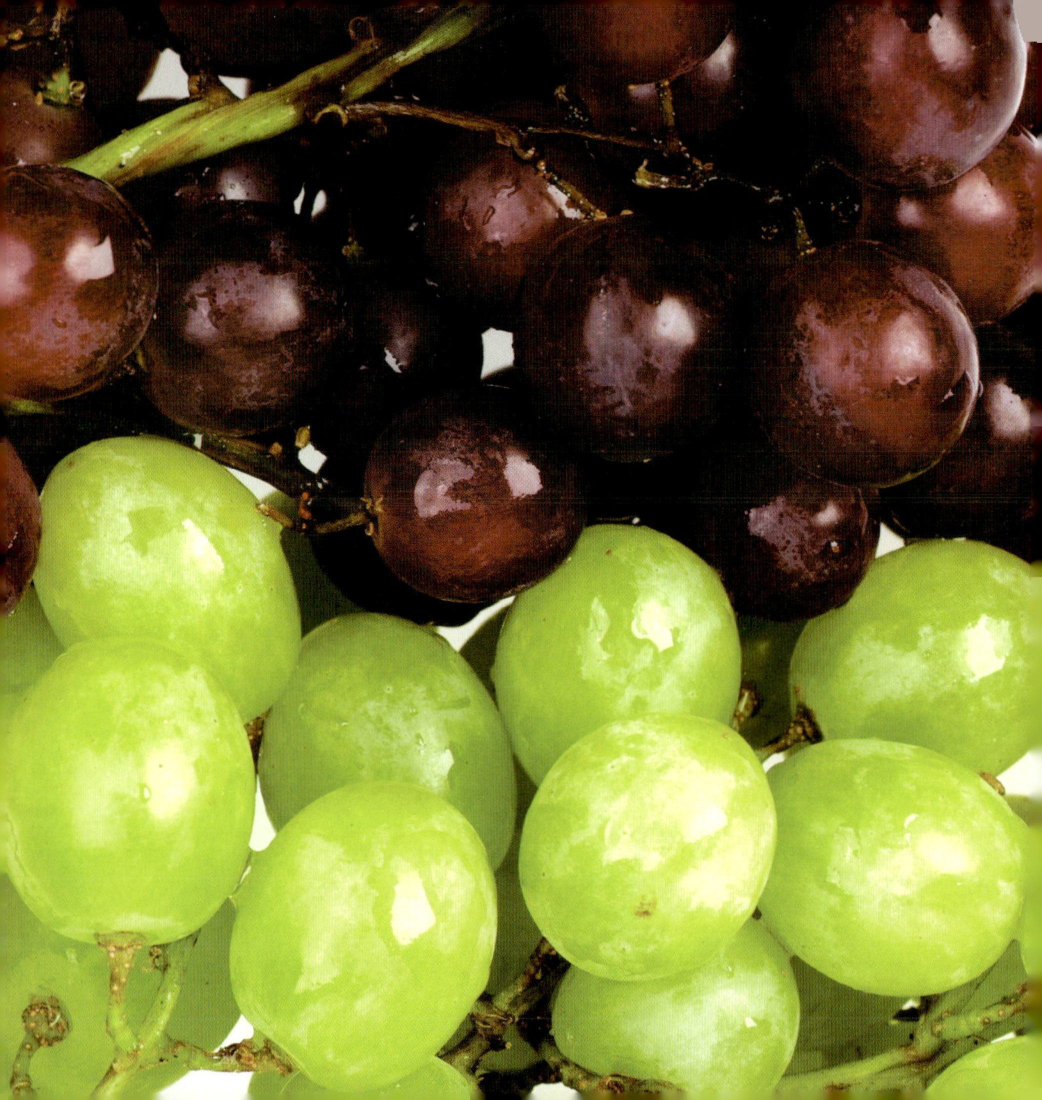

Vitis Vinifera

This is a pale yellow fixed oil, which has become very popular as a massage oil in recent times. It is extracted from grape pips but unfortunately great heat is used to obtain the oil. This effectively destroys any nutrients or vitamins and makes the oil worthless for therapeutic purposes. In the unlikely event that a source can be obtained from "cold-pressing," it is a light oil which is fairly neutral but can be drying on the skin.

Jasminum Officinalis

An orange liquid with a strong, heady, floral smell that is an anti-depressant and has a long reputation as an aphrodisiac. It can be very useful as a post-natal massage oil as it prevents uterine spasm and stimulates the flow of breast milk in nursing mothers. It also works on the respiratory system as an anti-spasmodic, relieving catarrh and colds. Beneficial for dry and sensitive skins.

jojoba

Simmondsia Chinensis

Jojoba is in fact a liquid wax extracted from the beans of the jojoba plant. It becomes quite solid at cool temperatures and is a pale yellow color. Its chemical composition is very similar to that of skin sebum and its anti-bacterial properties give it a long shelf life. Used extensively in the beauty industry, it is valuable on all types of skin as both a cleanser and a "wrinkle fighter!" It re-hydrates mature skin and is valuable in treating psoriasis and eczema. Commonly found in many commercial shampoos it is wonderful for hair. It is also thought to have some anti-inflammatory properties.

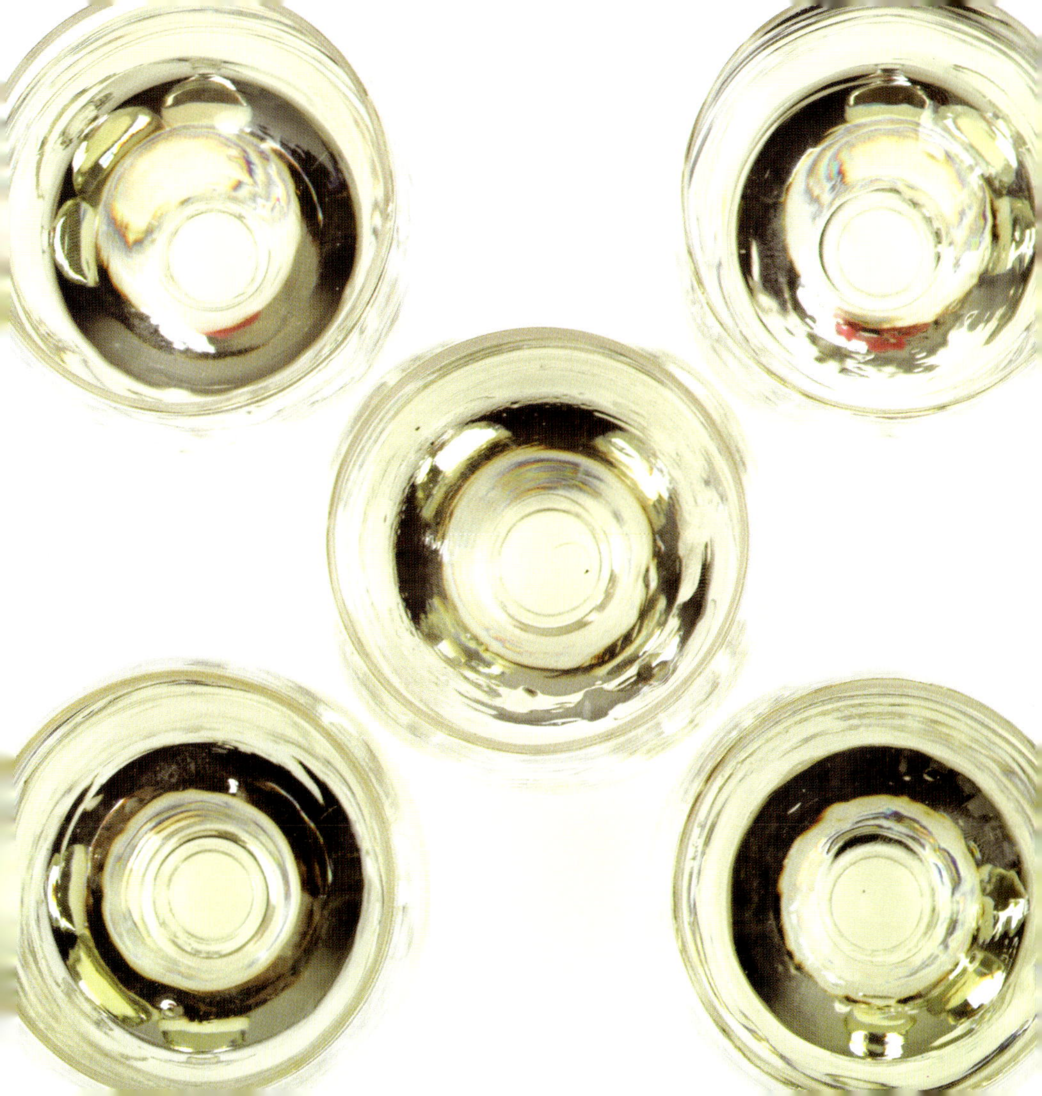

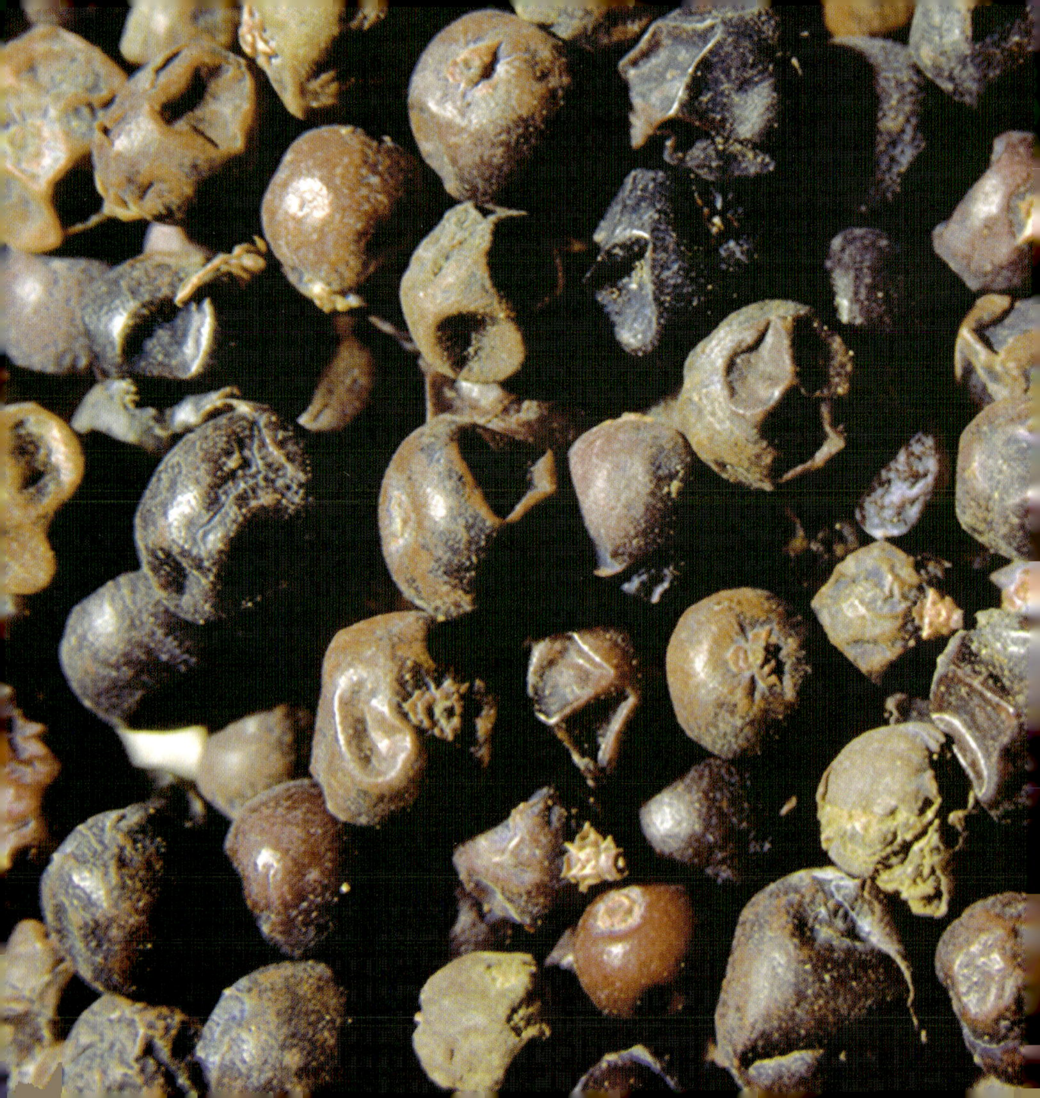

Juniperus Communis

This colorless oil is extracted from the berries and the main commercial use is for the flavoring of gin. Oils are also available from the needles and twigs but the way in which they are obtained can make them undesirable for therapeutic use. The oil is diuretic and useful in the treatment of arthritis and rheumatic conditions. It is beneficial for skin conditions including acne, oily skin, dry eczema, and dermatitis. A good general antiseptic with actions on the respiratory, digestive, and urinary tracts. Juniper is eliminated from the body via the kidneys but this can take some time. It is unwise therefore to use it for prolonged periods. Juniper blends well with the citrus oils, rose, clary sage, cypress, and geranium.

WARNING: This should be avoided completely during pregnancy.

lavender

Lavandula Angustifolia

A colorless oil with a sweet, woody and floral scent. This is probably the most familiar essential oil, and certainly the most popular. Unfortunately its popularity has made it quite difficult to obtain good-quality, unadulterated oil but it certainly is the one that every home should have. It has so many uses that a complete list is practically impossible but for the treatment of burns it is really special. As soon as a burn is cold, put lavender on it! Its healing properties are remarkable as it accelerates cell growth and repair. It is sedative and analgesic, and helps with high blood pressure, rheumatic pain, and muscular aches. Use it for insect bites, stings, dermatitis, dry eczema, abscesses, and acne. Also for headaches, depression and insomnia, migraine, blisters, and bruises. If you run out of things to try it on, it is even said to be an antidote to black widow spider venom! It blends with almost any other oil.

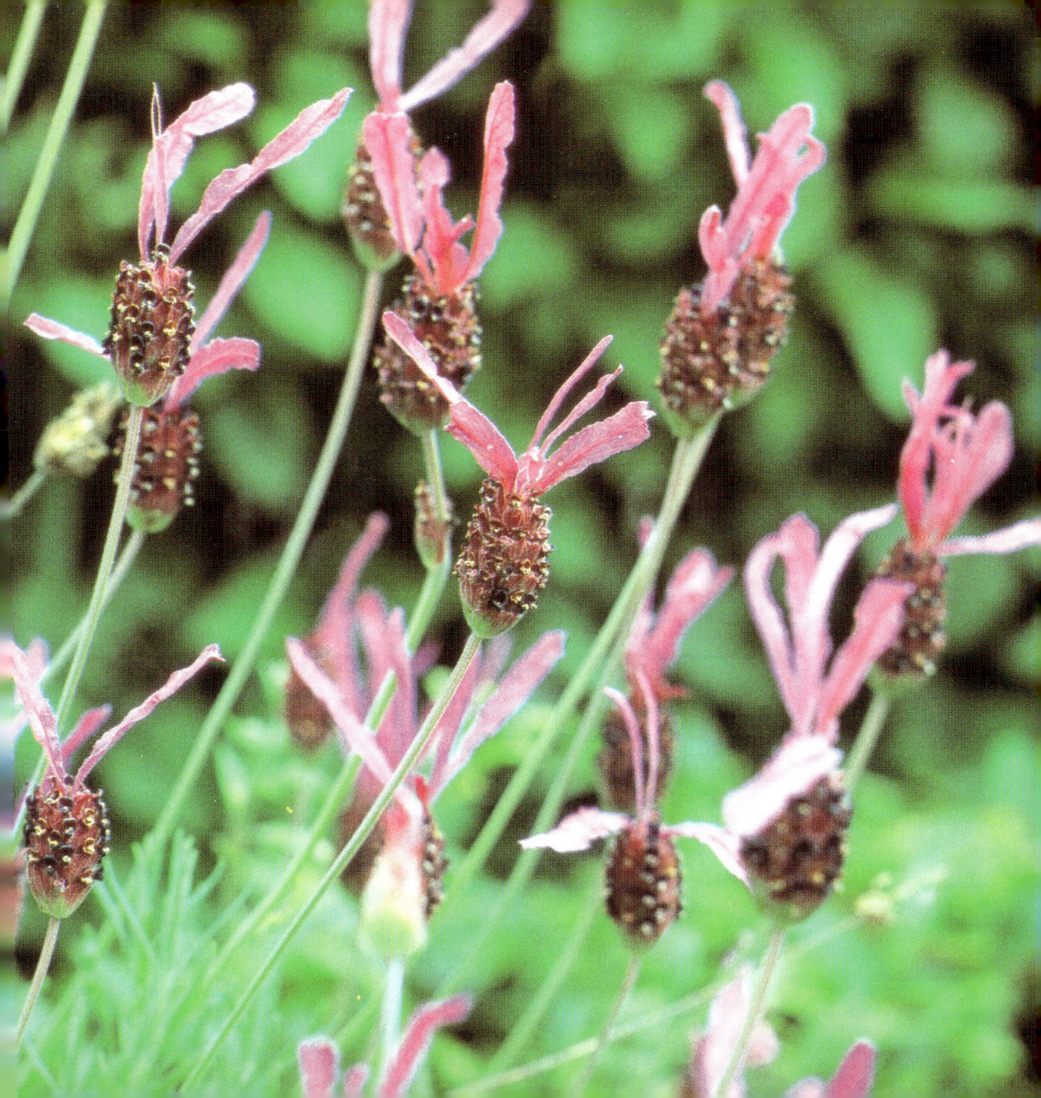

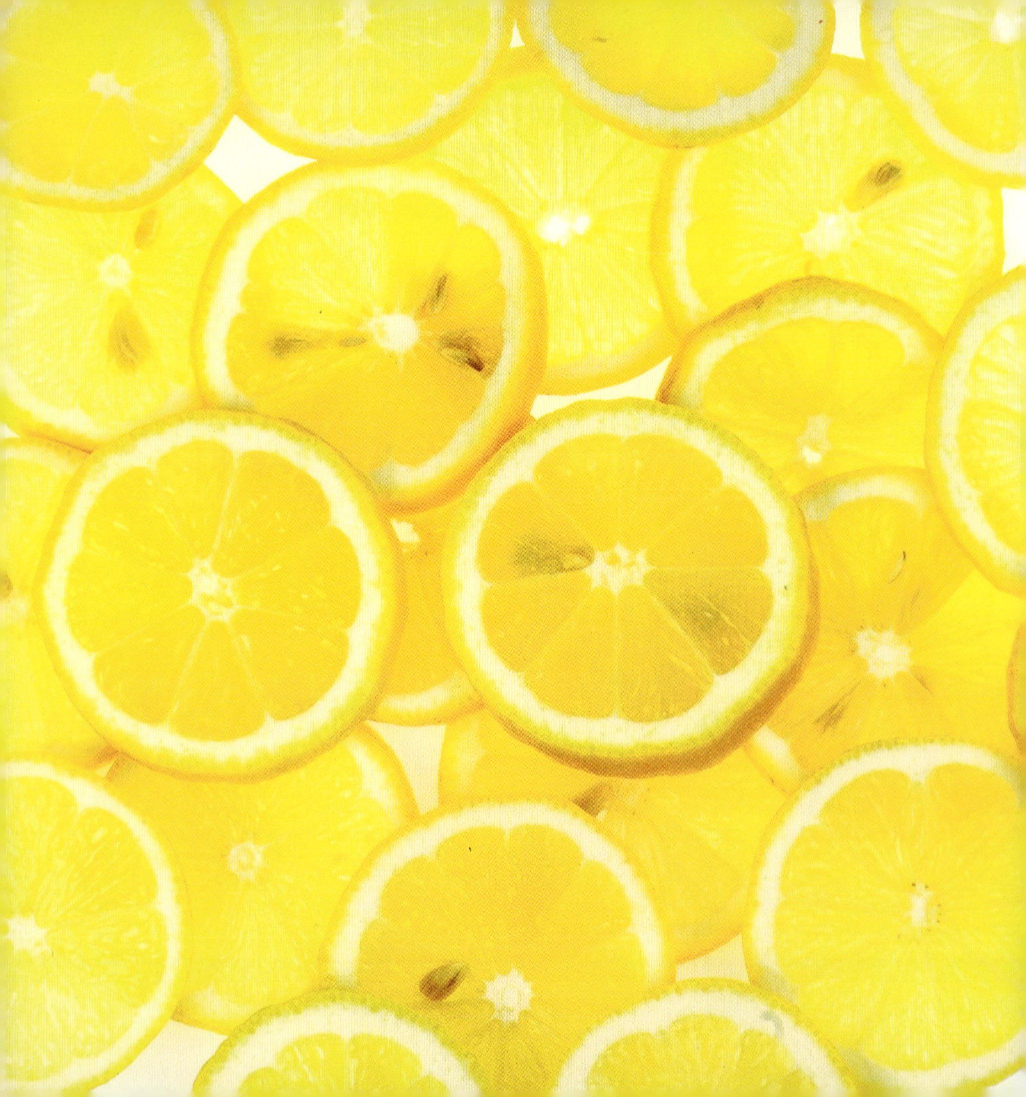

Citrus Limonum

Not surprisingly, this is a yellow oil that smells of lemons. It is a bright, cheerful oil obtained, like grapefruit, by expression from the peel. It is a good antiseptic and bactericide and its astringent properties make it useful for oily skin and brittle nails. It can help to disperse gall and kidney stones and is good for arthritis and rheumatism. You'll also find it worth putting in a blend for varicose veins. Insects do not like it. It blends well, although as with other citrus oils, be careful as it can make the skin more sensitive to ultraviolet light.

lemongrass

Cymbopogon Citratus

This oil is yellow and extracted from an oriental grass. It has a sharp smell very reminiscent of sherbet lemons. Lemongrass is quite a good "stress buster" and can be used for muscle spasm, palpitations, digestive disorders, enteritis, and colitis. It is another oil that stimulates breast milk in nursing mothers. A valuable insect repellent particularly for lice. It is a bactericide and a good antiseptic. With such a strong fragrance it can be difficult to blend but cypress or geranium mix well.

WARNING: Lemongrass can cause skin irritation in some people so use with care.

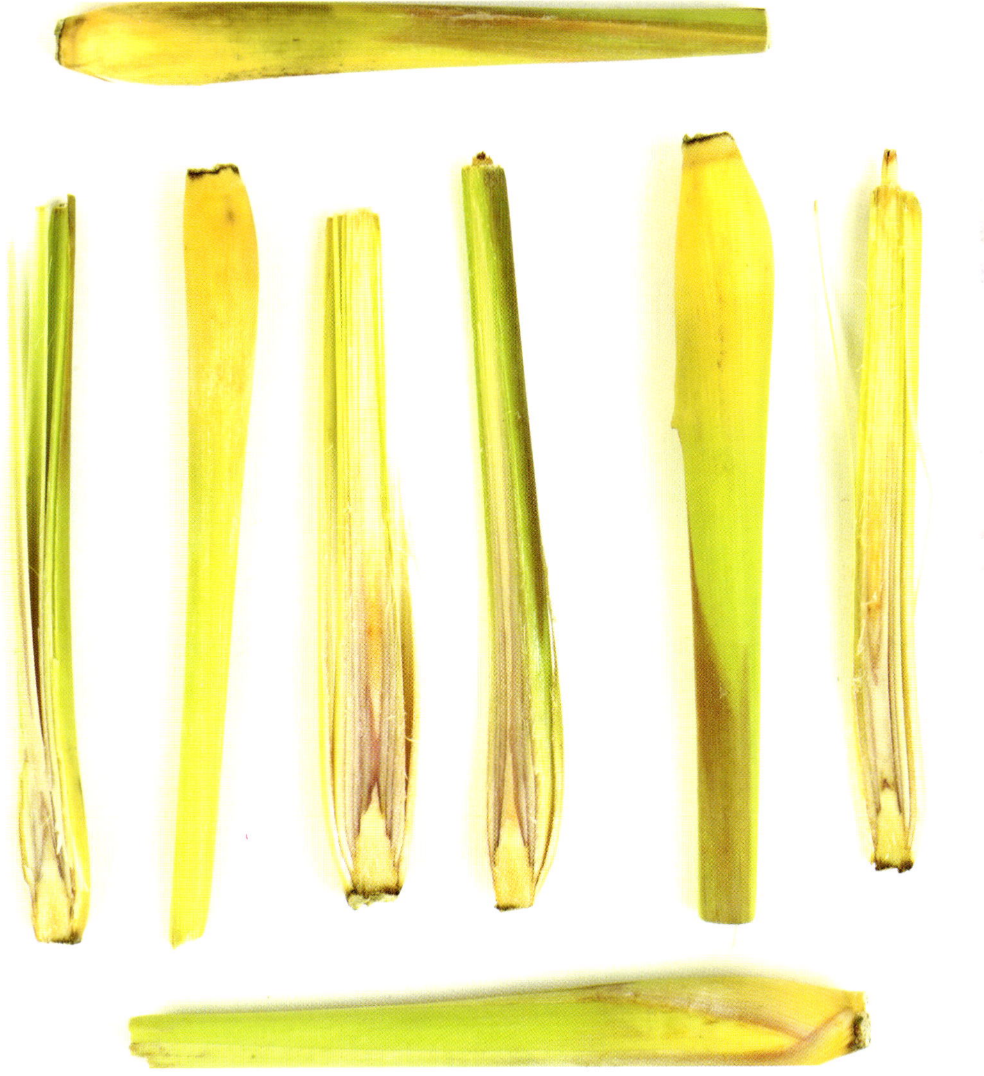

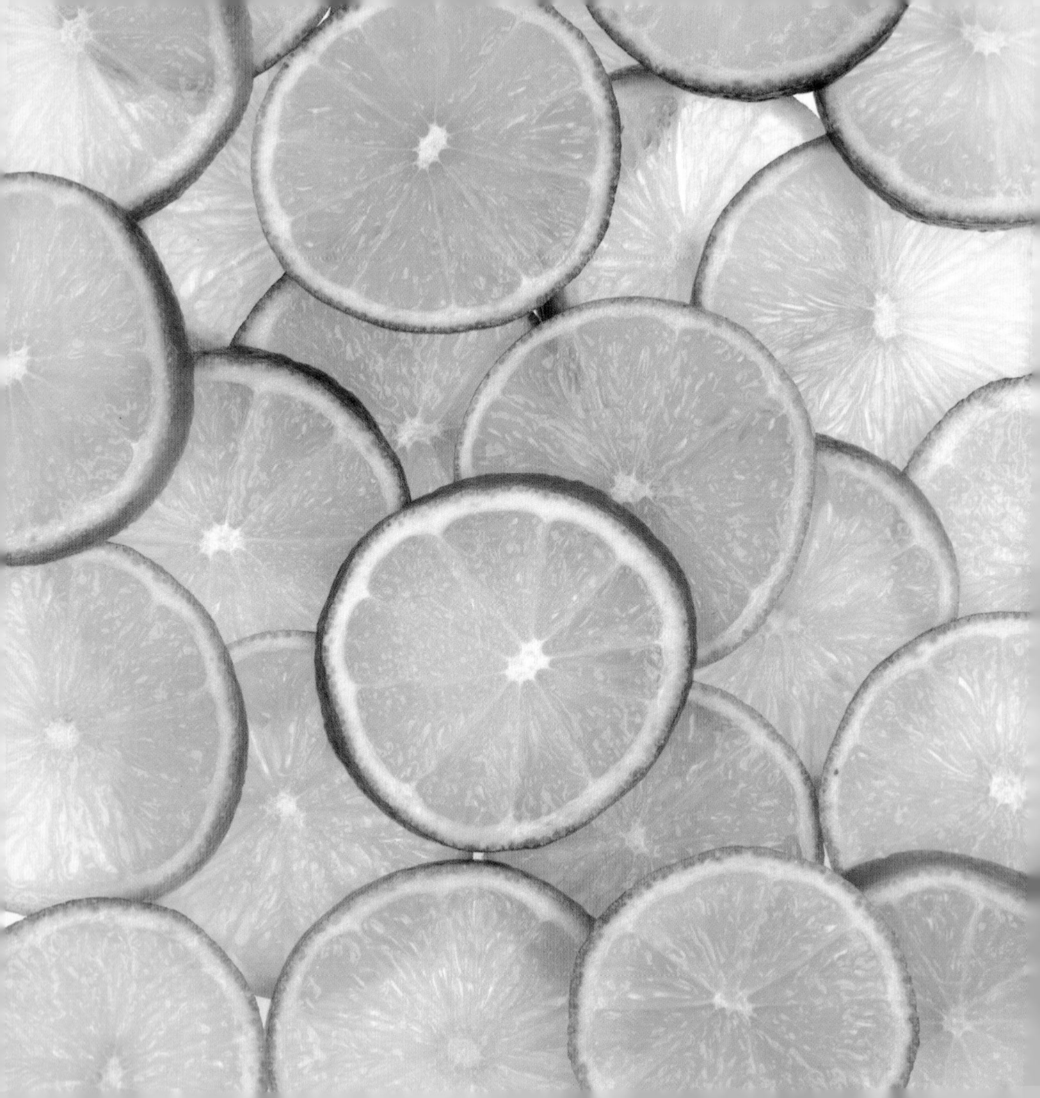

Citrus Aurantifolia

A delicious green oil with a rich, bright, fresh citrus smell. It is extracted by expression of the lime peel. The main use of this oil is actually for the food industry in the flavoring of soft drinks but it is also used in many cosmetics, soaps, and perfumes. Therapeutically, its uses are very similar to those of lemon oil but it does not have the same skin sensitivity problems. As with all citrus oils care must be taken with regard to increased sensitivity to ultraviolet light. Lime is an excellent oil for blending and its bright smell helps to clear the mind like a breath of fresh air.

Mandarin

Citrus Nobilis

Another oil which is an orange-yellow color, it is a little heavier in fragrance than the other citrus oils but still has a cheerful aspect. A wonderful oil for children's problems including digestive difficulties, colic, hiccups, and coughs. It is great for moms as well as it can help to get rid of stretch marks. You can use it for acne and oily skin. It is mildly diuretic and is used for obesity and fluid retention. It is another very good oil for blending but care with ultraviolet light is needed after application to the skin.

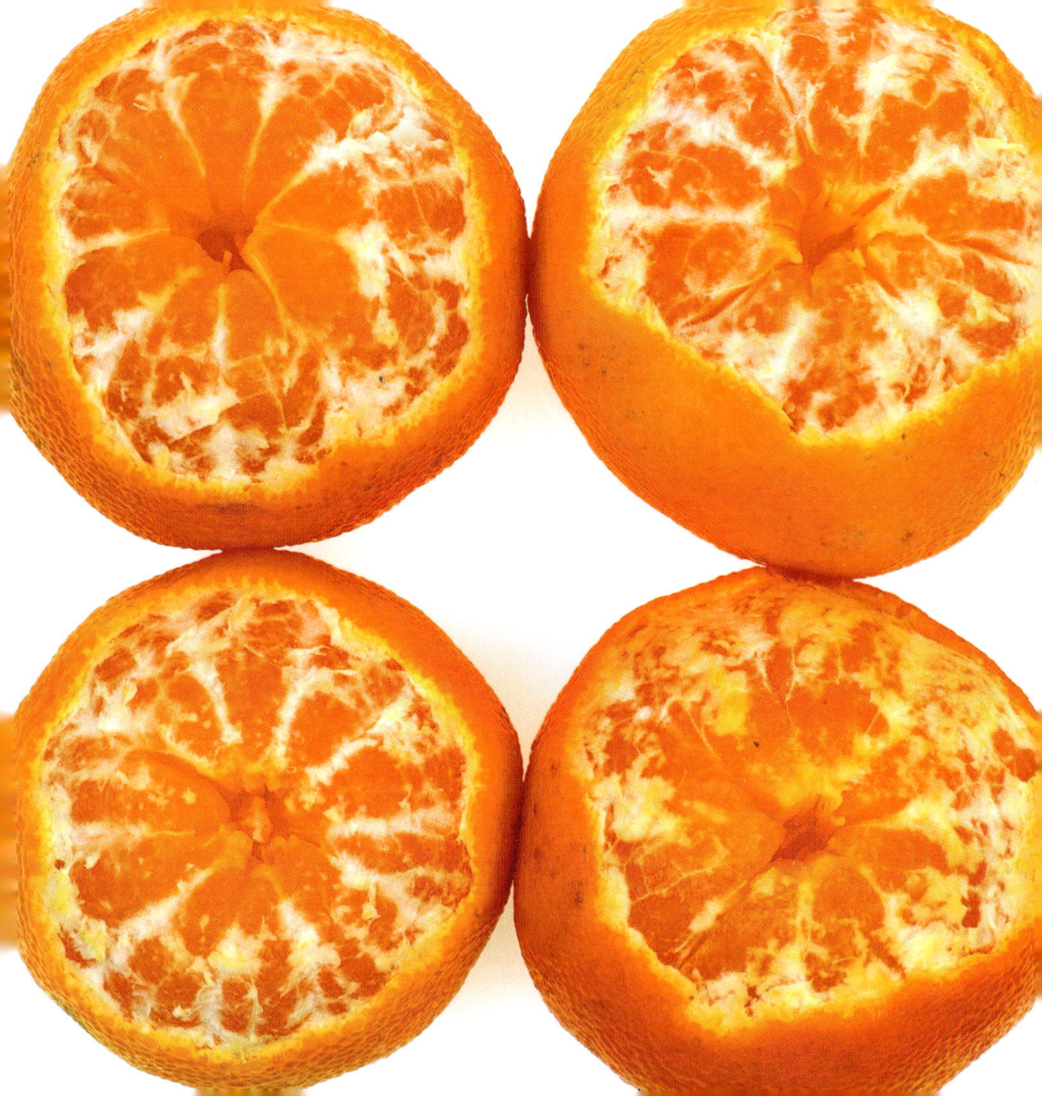

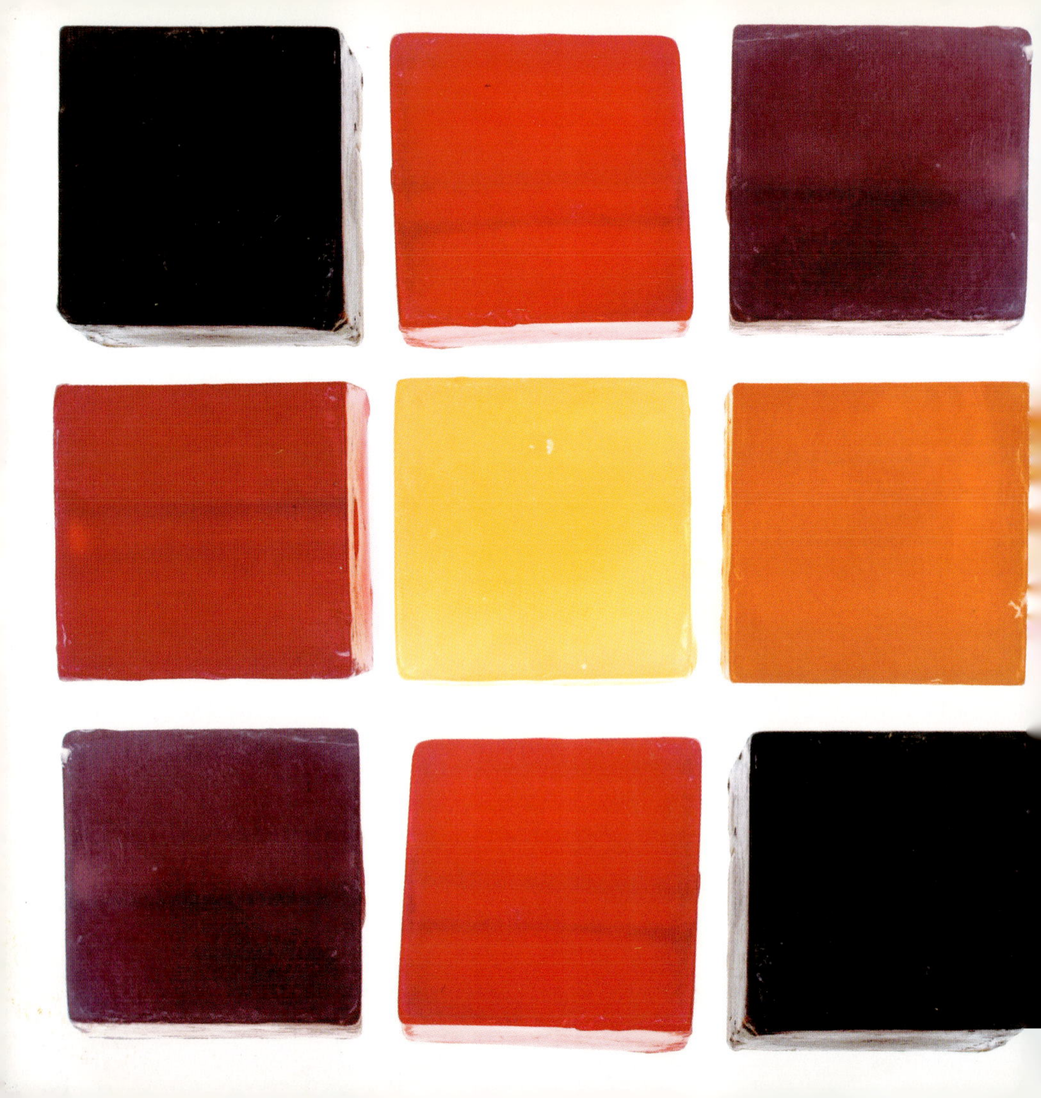

Origanum Marjorana

A yellow, brown oil with a herbaceous, warm and spicy smell. It is generally considered to be a sedative oil and can help significantly in lowering blood pressure. Muscle injuries, sprains, and strains will benefit from this oil and it helps to heal bruises. It can help greatly with sinus congestion, headaches, and colds. Insomnia sufferers can use marjoram to encourage sleep and it is safe for children to use as well, but only in tiny amounts. A little in a bath after a stressful day is well worth trying. It can even help to get rid of ticks on cats and dogs!

myrrh

Commiphora Myrrha

This is an amber-colored oil which nearly everyone has heard of but few have smelled. It has a strange smoky, balsamic scent and is quite warm to the nose. Featuring strongly in the Bible, it has been valued for centuries. Wounds that are difficult to heal including ulcers, bed sores, and even gangrene can harness myrrh oil's ability to preserve flesh and aid the healing process. A couple of drops in a mouthwash will help gingivitis and mouth ulcers but make sure you spit it out after a rinse as it tastes awful. Good for athlete's foot and candida, coughs and colds, asthma, and sore throats. It stimulates the flow of gastric juice and so is an excellent aid to the digestive system. Myrrh tends to get very thick and sticky as it ages and can glue the top on the bottle but it lasts for years. Taking over 24 hours to be eliminated from the body, it should not be used for prolonged periods. It does not blend well but combines reasonably with lavender.

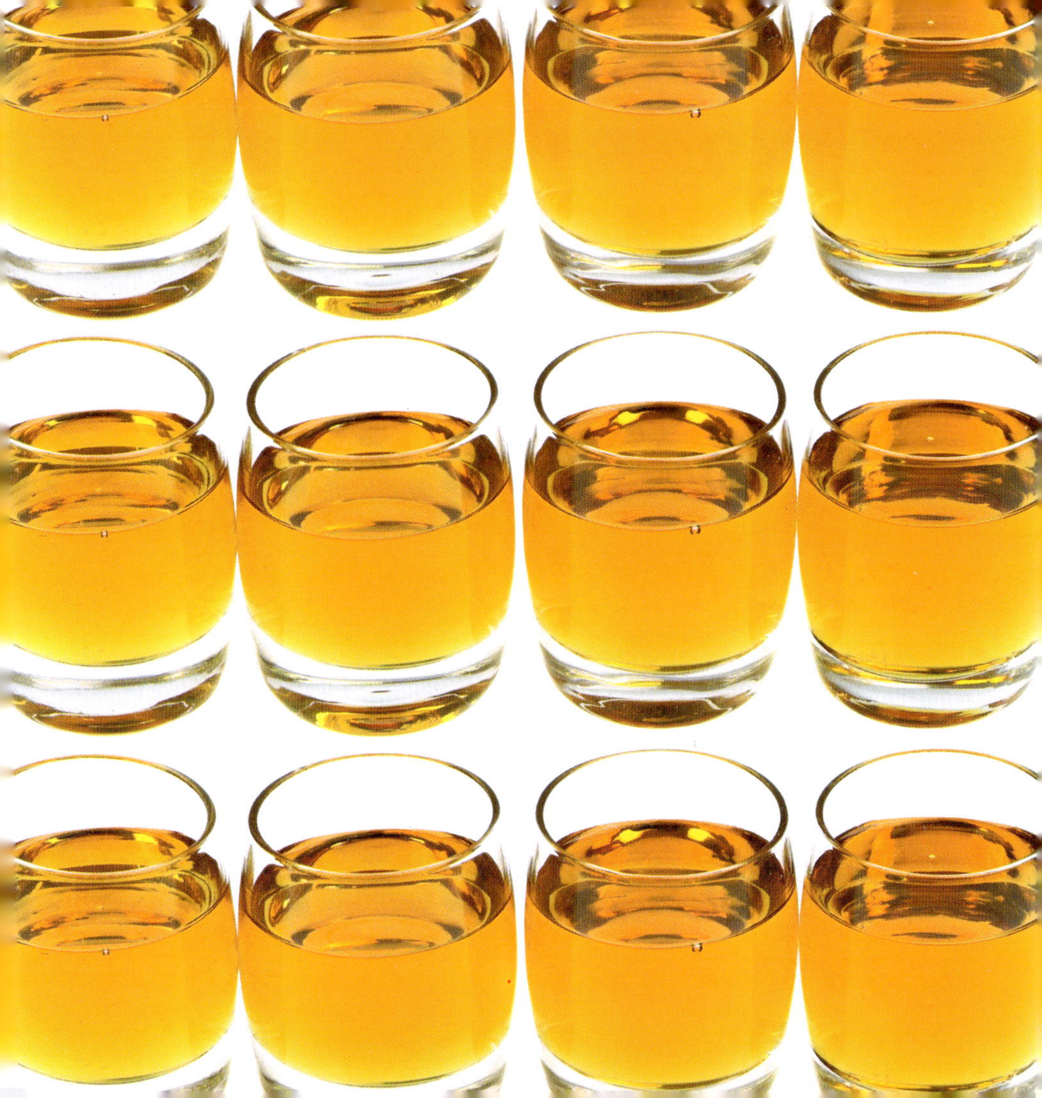

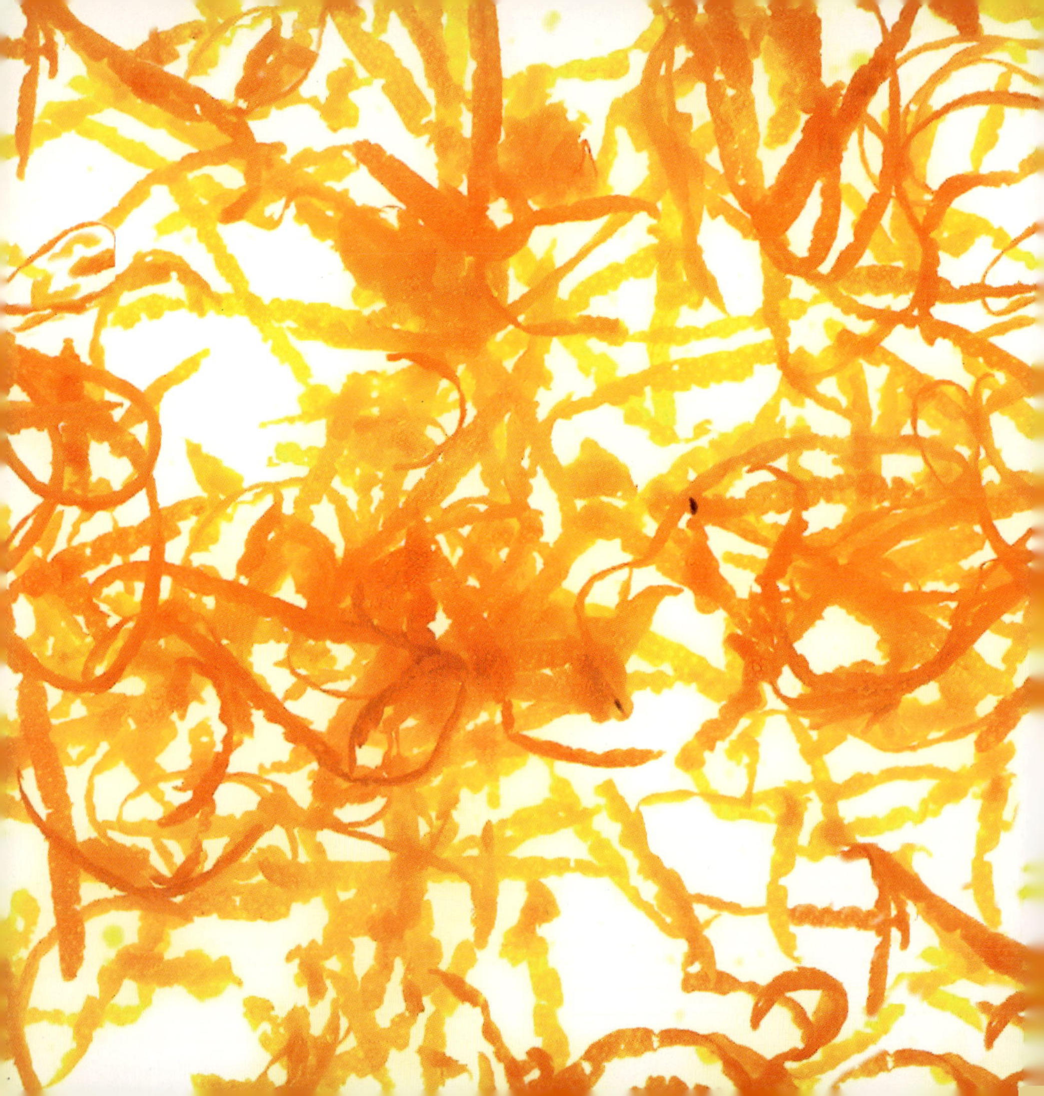

Citrus Aurantium

A pale yellow oil with a light, refreshing, floral smell extracted from the flowers of the bitter orange tree, it has a long reputation as an aphrodisiac. As a valued and highly utilized ingredient in the perfume industry, neroli commands a very high price. It is arguably the best stress remedy oil available as it calms the mind and helps with anxiety. Good for heart palpitations and muscle spasm, it can assist with chronic shock, particularly post-operative shock. It is excellent for skin care, especially for dry and irritable skin, broken capillaries, and stretch marks. It blends well with many oils but use it with care, it is very expensive!

niaouli

Melaleuca Viridiflora

This pale yellow oil has a strong camphoraceous smell. Its main use is for bronchial conditions including coughs, colds, sore throats, and bronchitis. You can also find it listed as an ingredient in toothpastes, mouth washes and cough medicines. It has been used in French hospitals as an antiseptic and before that to purify water. Good for urinary infections, rheumatism, indigestion, insect bites, wounds, and acne. More recently it has been valuable in the treatment of radiotherapy burns following cancer treatment.

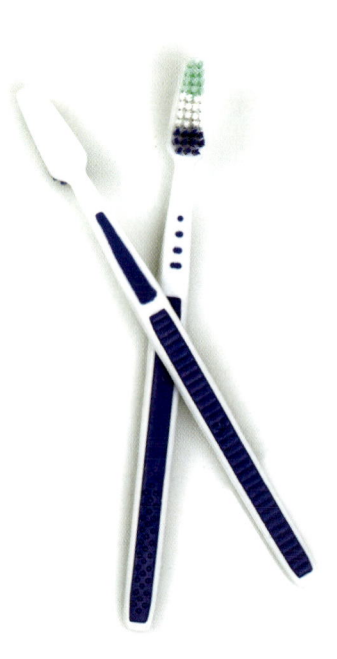

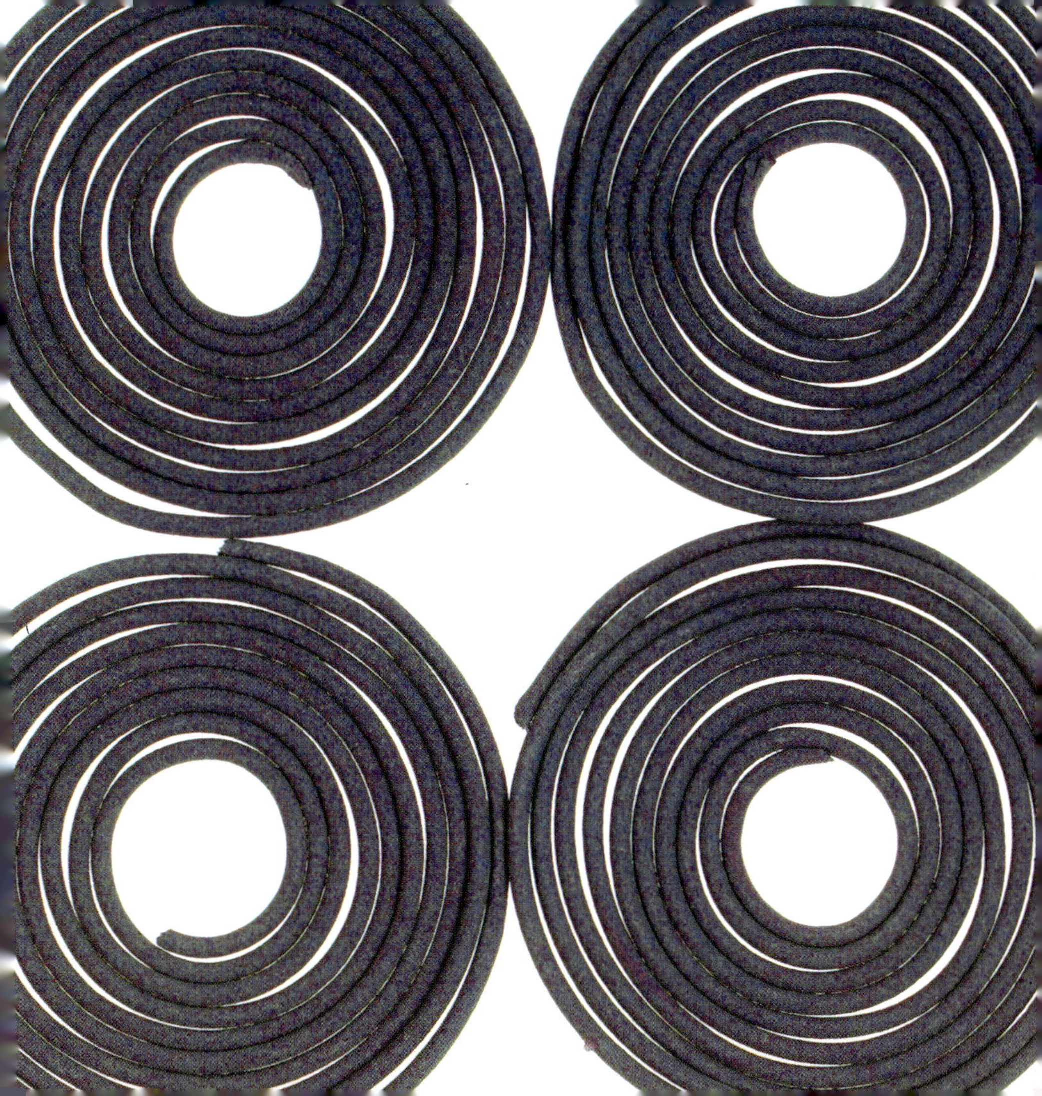

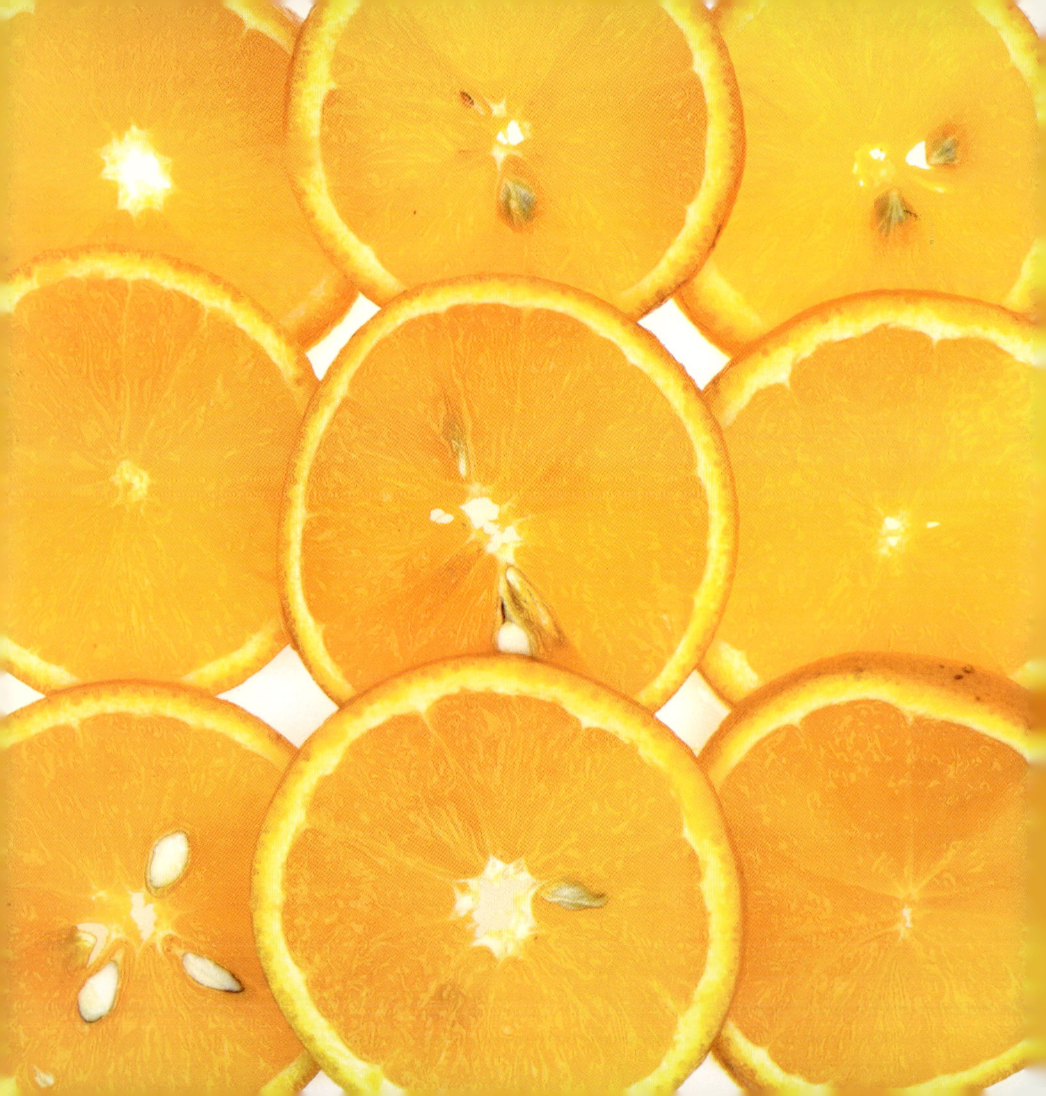

Citrus Sinensis

This yellow oil is extracted from the peel of the sweet orange and huge amounts are used in the food industry and in the production of soft drinks. Unsurprisingly, it has a lovely scent of oranges and has recently become very popular as a household cleaning product. Therapeutically, it is good for oily skins and acne and helps to lower high blood pressure. Used to balance the digestive system, it can relieve both constipation and diarrhea. A useful oil for fluid retention and for colds and influenza. The usual care must be taken with regard to exposure to ultraviolet light. You will find it is an excellent blender.

palmarosa

Cymbopogon Martini

This is another pale yellow oil extracted from a grass. With a sweet, gentle, geranium-like smell, it helps to balance sebum production in the skin making it useful for oily skin, acne, and dermatitis. Valuable for intestinal infections and candida as it helps to balance the intestinal bacteria, also it works well as an antiseptic and helps wounds to heal quickly. It can also help with nervous exhaustion and stress-related conditions. It blends well with cedarwood, lavender, and ylang ylang.

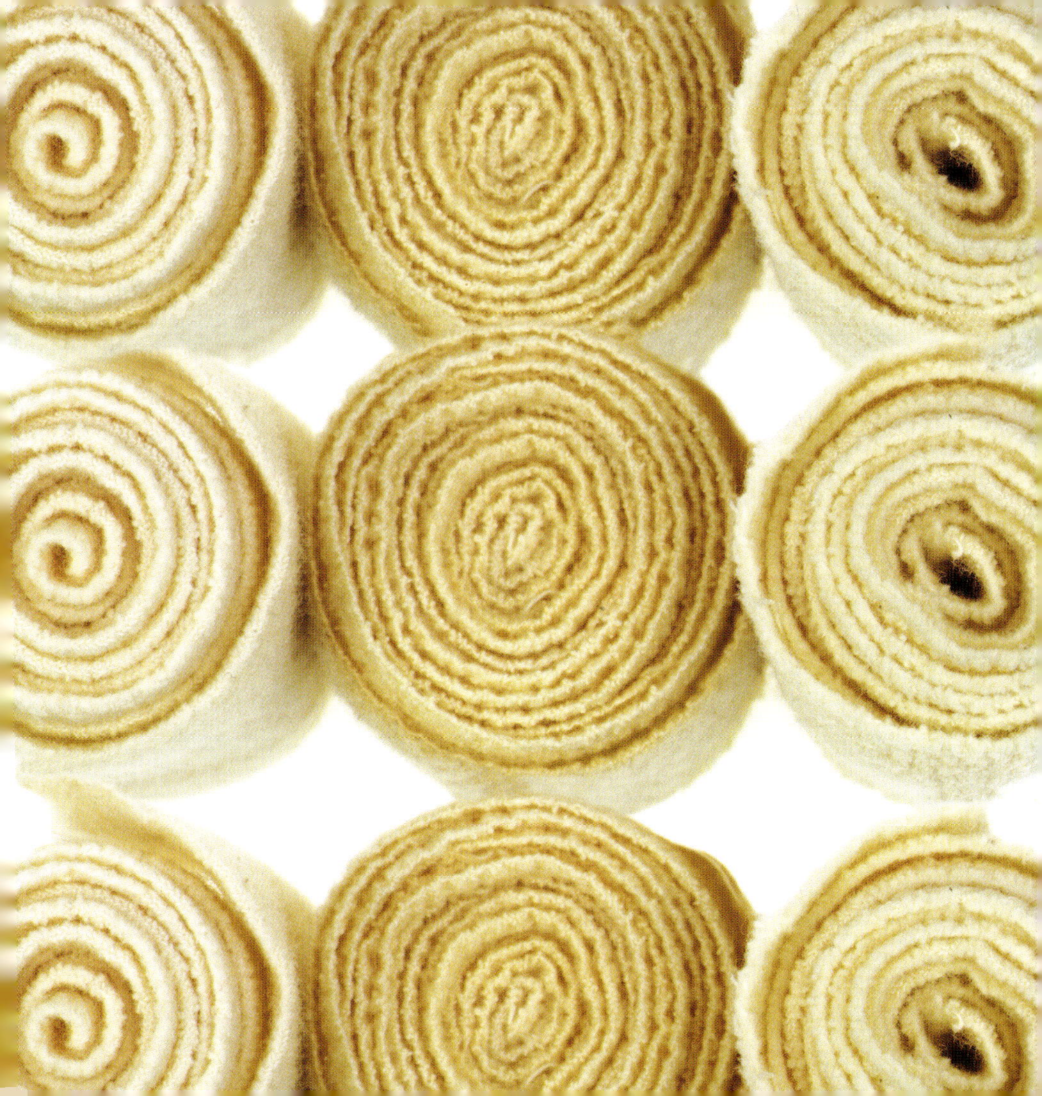

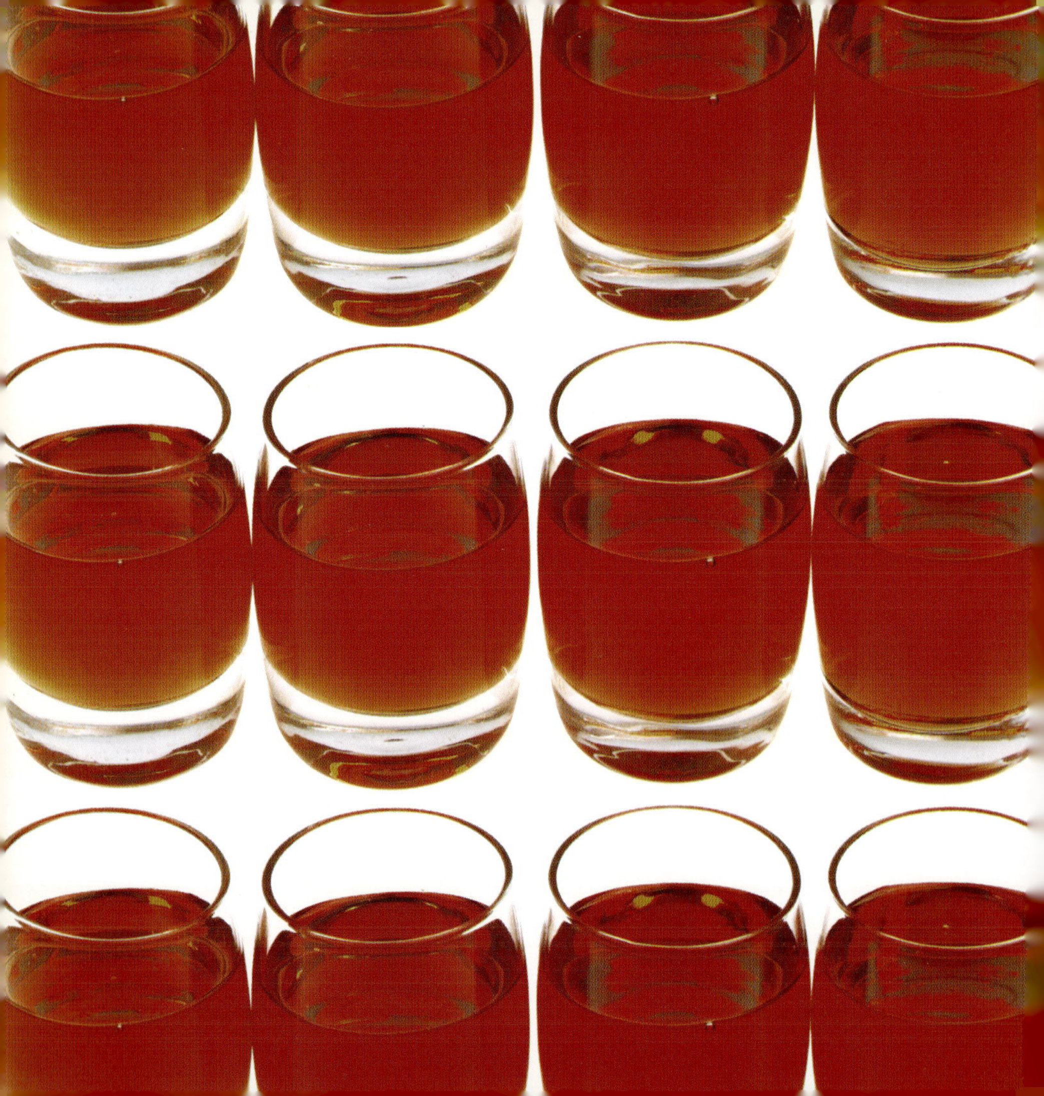

Pogostemon Cablin

A reddish brown oil with a sweet, heavy and musty aroma, it is unusual in the world of essential oils in that it improves with age. It is not to everyone's taste as it is quite "clingy" and a difficult fragrance to remove or hide. However, it is reputed to be an aphrodisiac and an anti-depressant. Use it to help heal long-term wounds and for skin care problems including acne, dermatitis, and weeping eczema. Also good for athlete's foot and verrucae. It can help with nausea and travel sickness. Care is needed in blending as it has a very powerful aroma.

peach kernel

Prunus Persica

This is a luxurious carrier oil with a smooth texture, golden color and faint peach aroma. It is quite expensive and is extracted by expression from the kernels. It is a wonderful base oil for facial massage as it encourages the skin to secrete its own natural oils and prevent dehydration. It keeps the skin supple and elastic and is very good for sensitive complexions. It also promotes hair shine and texture if a little is added to shampoo. It can easily be mixed with other base oils.

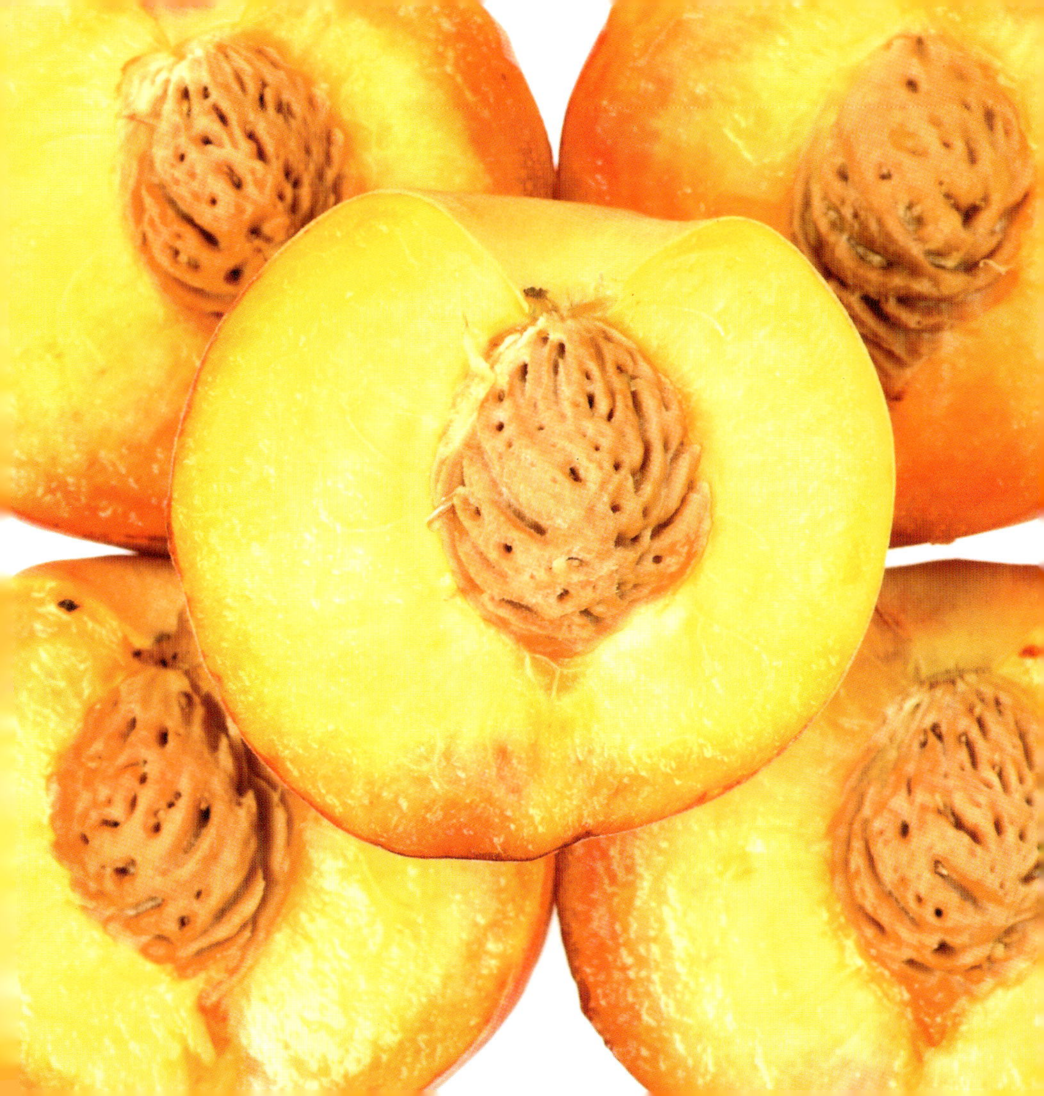

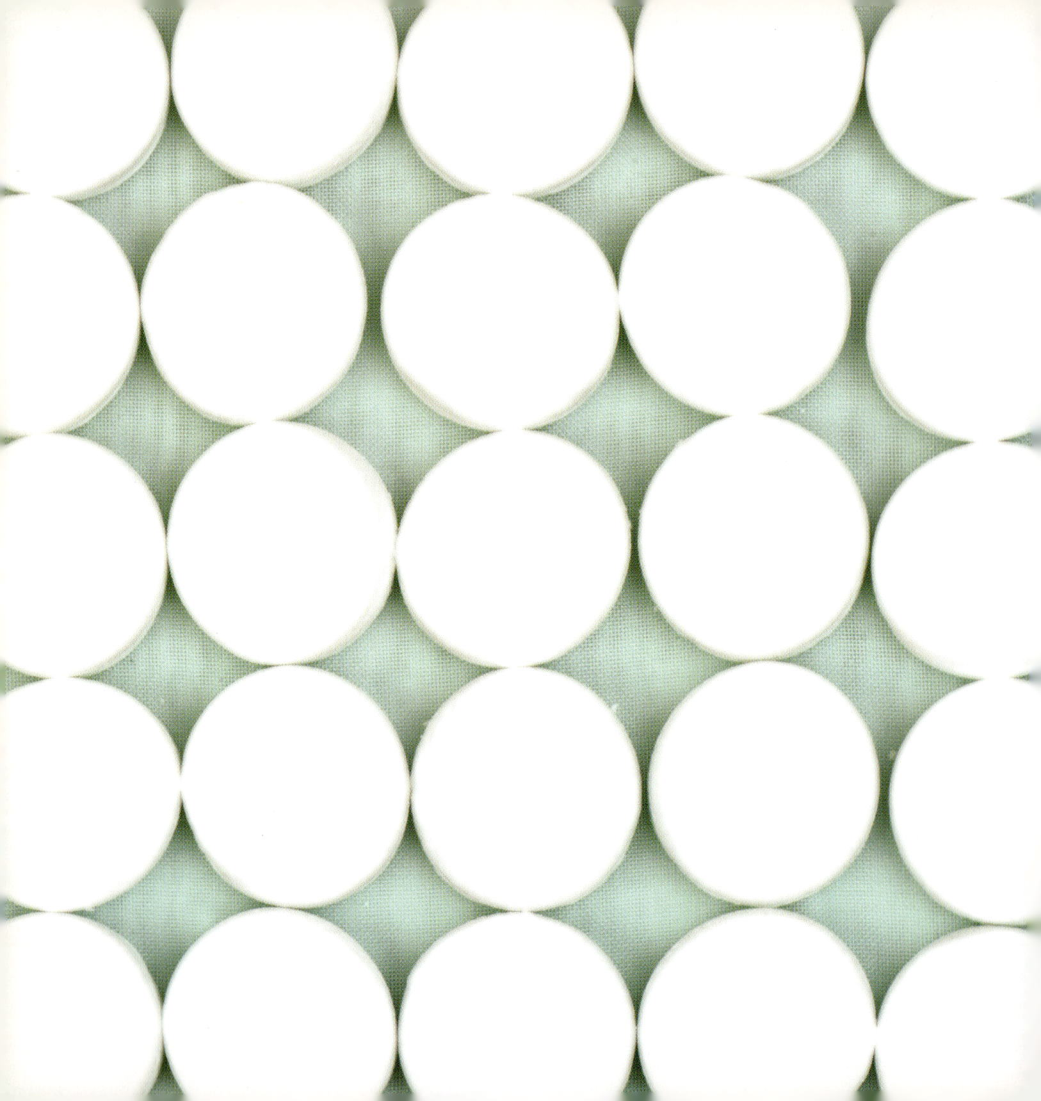

Mentha Piperita

A very pale yellow oil with an unmistakable smell of menthol which, unfortunately, is sometimes sold alone instead of the whole oil. Everyone must be familiar with its reputation for assisting the digestive system and its use for indigestion, flatulence, colic, nausea and diarrhea, irritable bowel syndrome, and colitis. It is also useful for respiratory conditions including coughs, sinus congestion, and congestive headaches. It does stop the flow of breast milk in nursing mothers. However it is a wonderful mosquito and rat repellent! Care should be taken as at low dilutions it can stop skin irritation whereas at high concentrations it can cause irritation. The oil should not be used on young children or people taking homeopathic medicines.

petitgrain

Citrus Aurantium

Another pale yellow oil extracted from the bitter orange tree but this time from the leaves and twigs. Much cheaper than neroli oil and more delicate in its fragrance, it is a good anti-depressant and useful in cases of anxiety. People convalescing from illness and from nervous exhaustion may also benefit from this oil's properties. Petitgrain is a good balancing oil as it is neither stimulating nor sedating and blends well with clary sage, geranium, lavender, and rosemary. It is recommended for acne, greasy skin and hair, and for excessive perspiration.

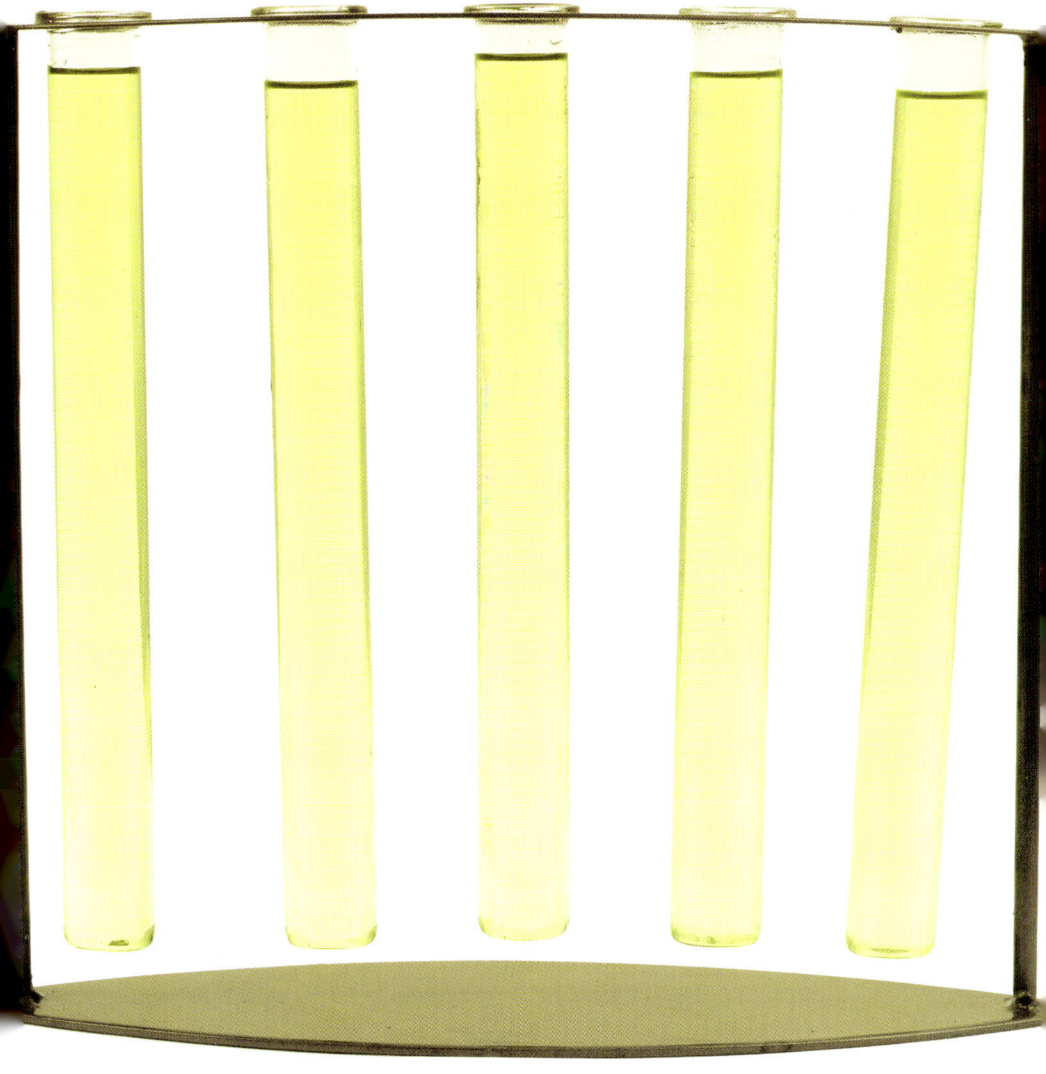

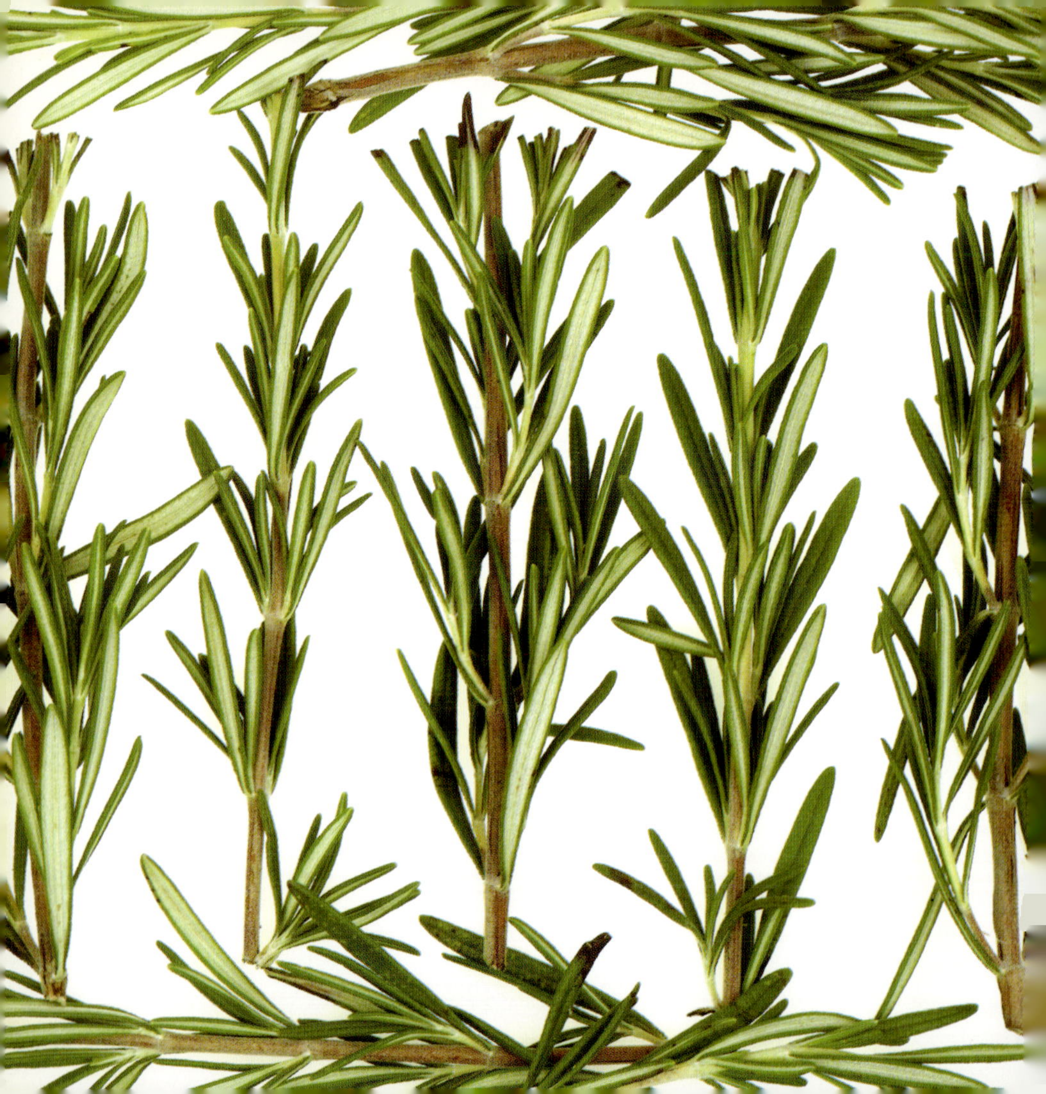

Rosmarinus Officinalis

A colorless oil with a sharp, camphoraceous aroma. Its Latin name means "dew of the sea" as it is a Mediterranean coastal plant. Working as a stimulating oil, particularly of the nervous system, it can be used on all types of muscle aches and pains, rheumatism, and arthritis. Used as a classic remedy for fainting and headaches, it can also help clear your head. Often added to shampoo to give life and luster to hair, it helps to prevent dandruff. When mixed with lemongrass it makes an excellent remedy for headlice.

WARNING: Avoid during pregnancy. Care is needed with people suffering from epilepsy.

rose otto

Rosa Damascena

The name for this queen of essential oils derives from "attar of roses." A colorless liquid is distilled from rose petals, which becomes quite solid at cool temperatures. Many imitations are sold as pure rose otto, but the real oil is incredibly expensive and there is no real substitute. It works to regulate female problems including irregular menstruation, discharges, and PMS, and helps impotence in men. Particularly effective in skin care, it has a wonderful soothing action on the nervous system. Blend it with frankincense for a cozy sensation. The expensive end of the perfume industry uses rose otto extensively, which plays a large part in dictating the price—along with the minute amounts of oil obtained from each blossom. It is worth its weight in gold so use it sparingly.

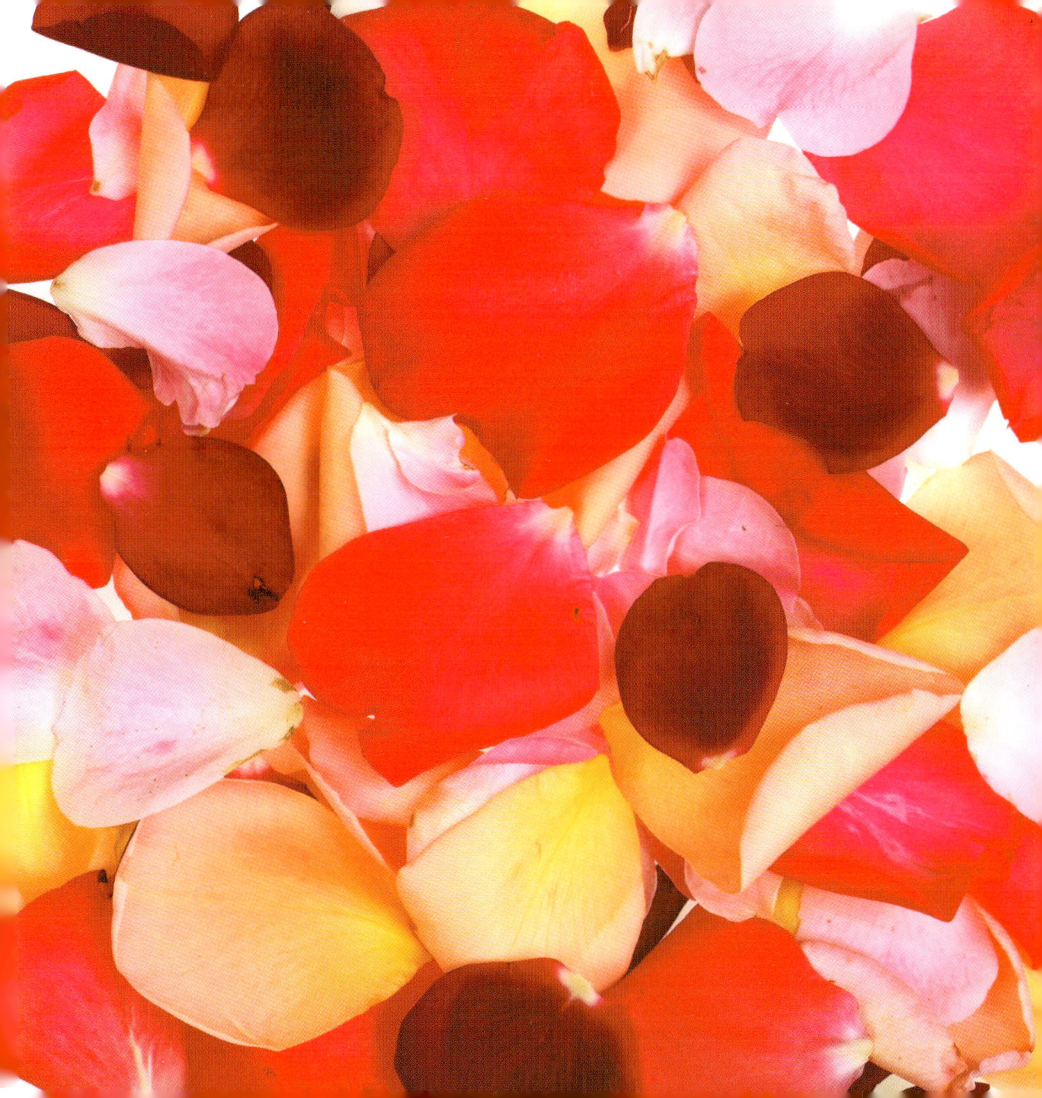

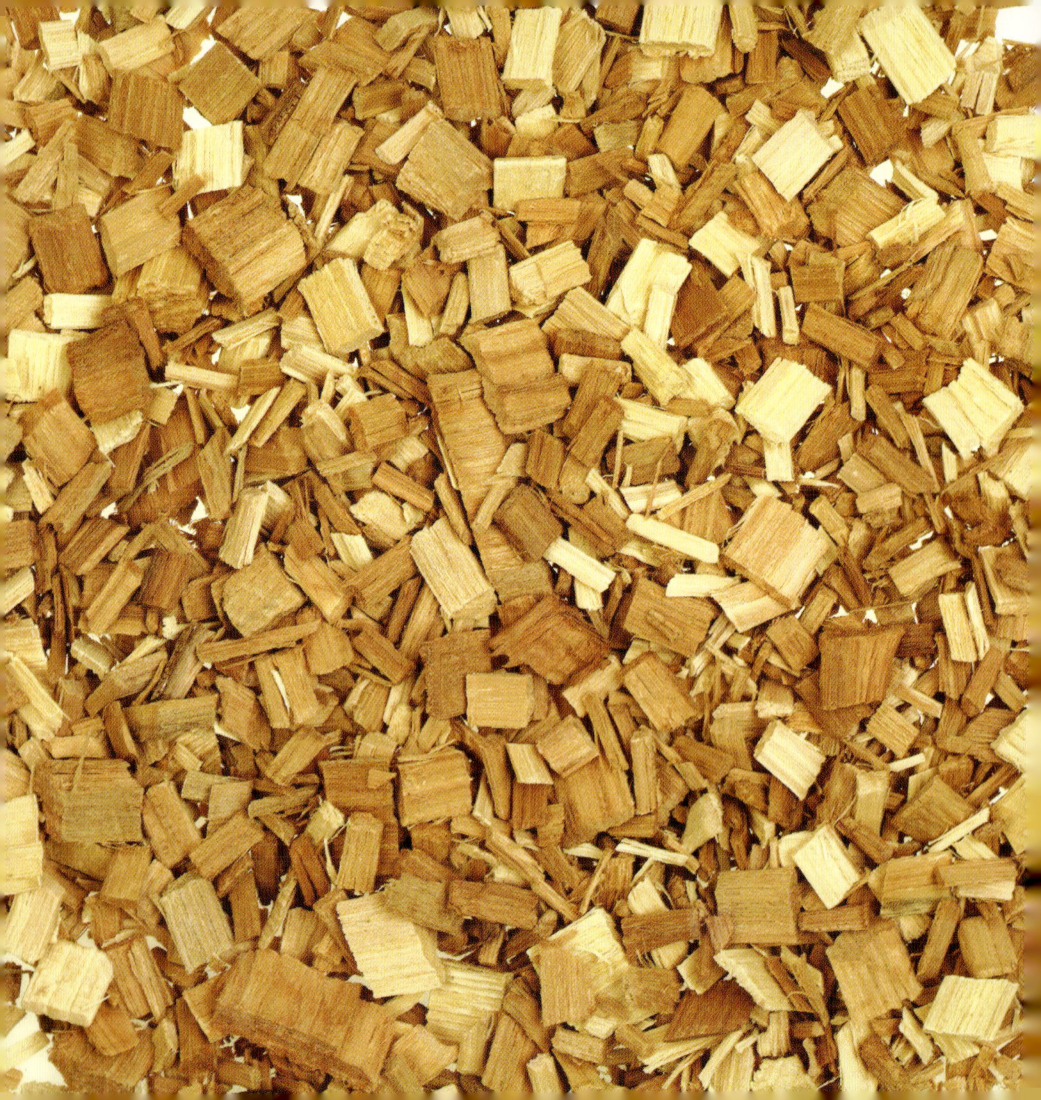

Aniba Rosaeodora

This oil is extracted from the wood chippings of the rosewood tree to produce a lovely soft, woody oil. Unfortunately, the tree comes from tropical rain forests and not all the oil available comes from renewable sources. The oil has noticeably uplifting effects and it works as a wonderful anti-depressant. It also helps to rejuvenate the skin and is particularly effective on mature, wrinkled, or sensitive skin. Rosewood oil is a good natural deodorant and has an analgesic effect on headaches. It is believed to help boost the immune system and prevent colds, influenza, and diseases; it blends well with most oils.

sandalwood

Santalum Album

This is a thick, sticky, yellow oil with a soft, sweet, and woody fragrance extracted by distillation from the tree. It can be an expensive oil as the amount available is strictly controlled. With pronounced anti-inflammatory and analgesic actions on the respiratory and urinary tracts, it can be used for colic, diarrhea, nausea, catarrh, laryngitis, and sore throats. For the skin it is valuable for dry, inflamed, and irritable skin, acne, and boils. It is considered by many to be an aphrodisiac. Sandalwood blends well with many oils and can be used as a fixative for perfumes.

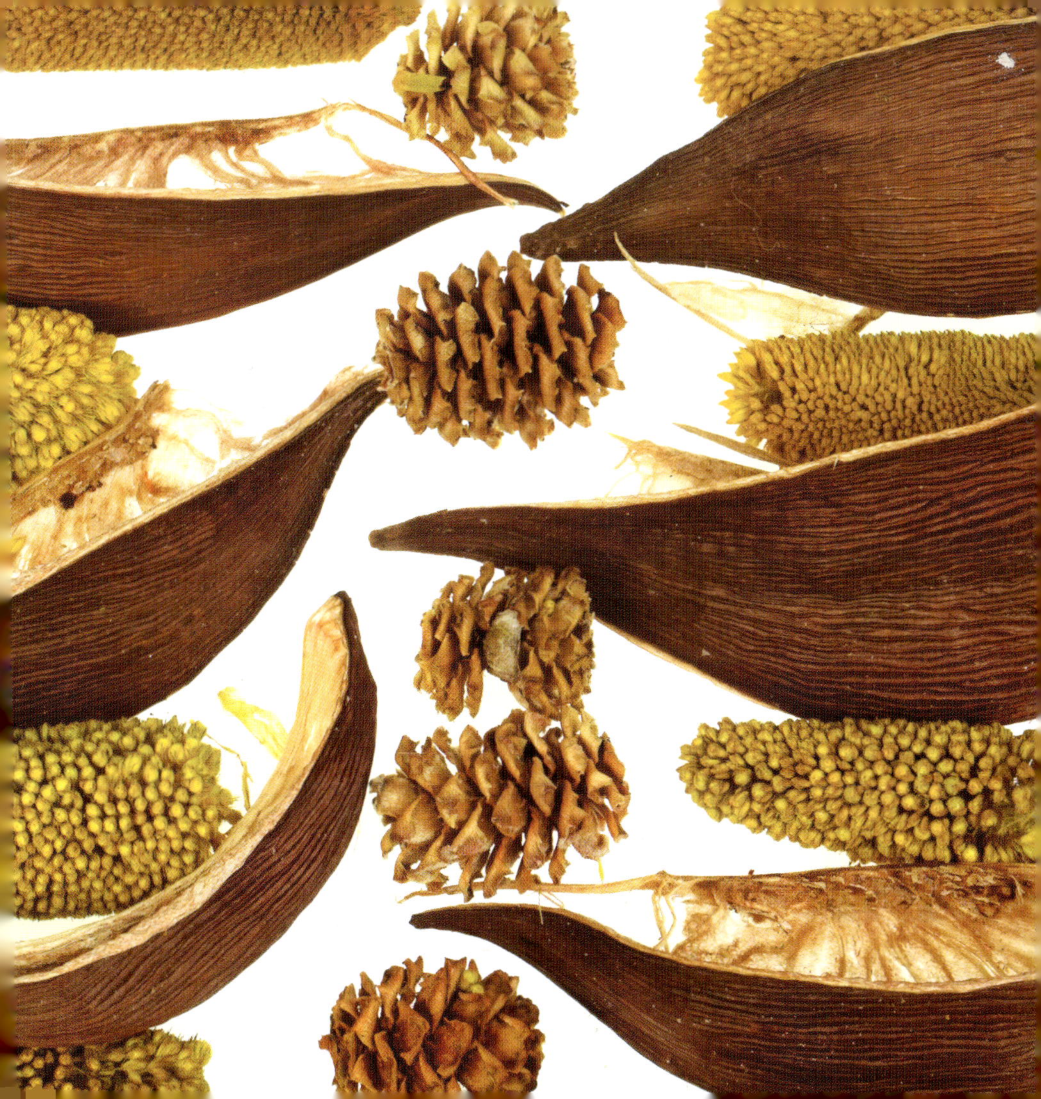

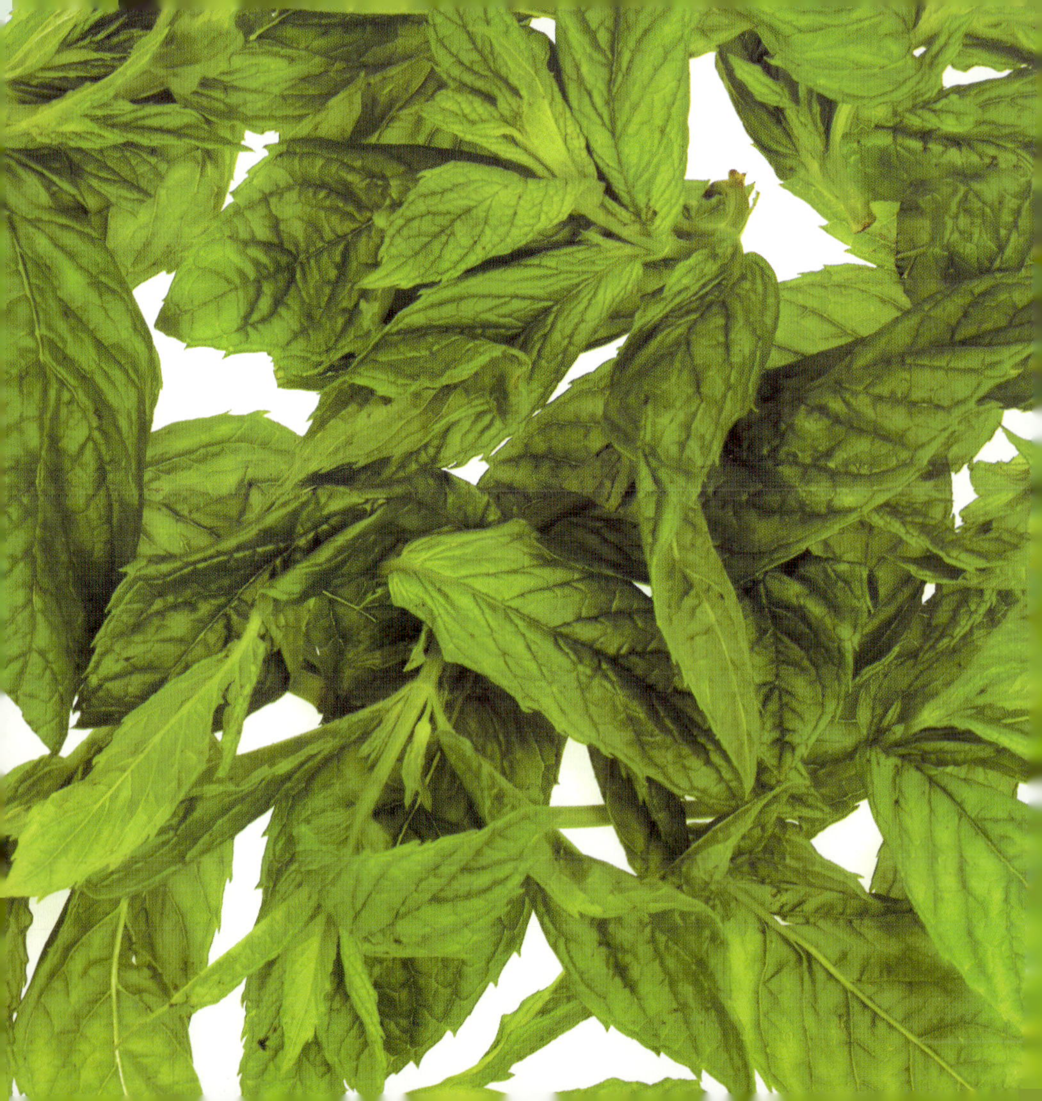

Mentha Spicata

This is a pale yellow oil with a warm, herbaceous, minty scent. Its properties are similar to peppermint but it is more suitable for children. It is useful in helping with acne and dermatitis, asthma, bronchitis, and catarrh. It is also good for digestive disorders including colic, flatulence, and nausea and has value in treating headaches and migraine. A great deal is used in the manufacture of toothpaste, chewing gum, and candy. It blends well with basil, eucalyptus, and rosemary.

sweet almond

Prunus Dulcis

This carrier oil is probably the most popular base oil for massage use. It is extracted by expression of almonds to give a pale yellow, fairly light, nearly odorless oil ideal for the addition of essential oils. With a number of vitamins it is very nourishing for dry skin. Anti-inflammatory properties make it valuable for psoriasis, eczema, and dermatitis. It can also be useful in relieving sunburn. Make the effort to find a good source of this oil as some is now obtained using a heating process which destroys the vitamins and nutritional qualities. The cold-pressed oil has a comparatively long shelf life.

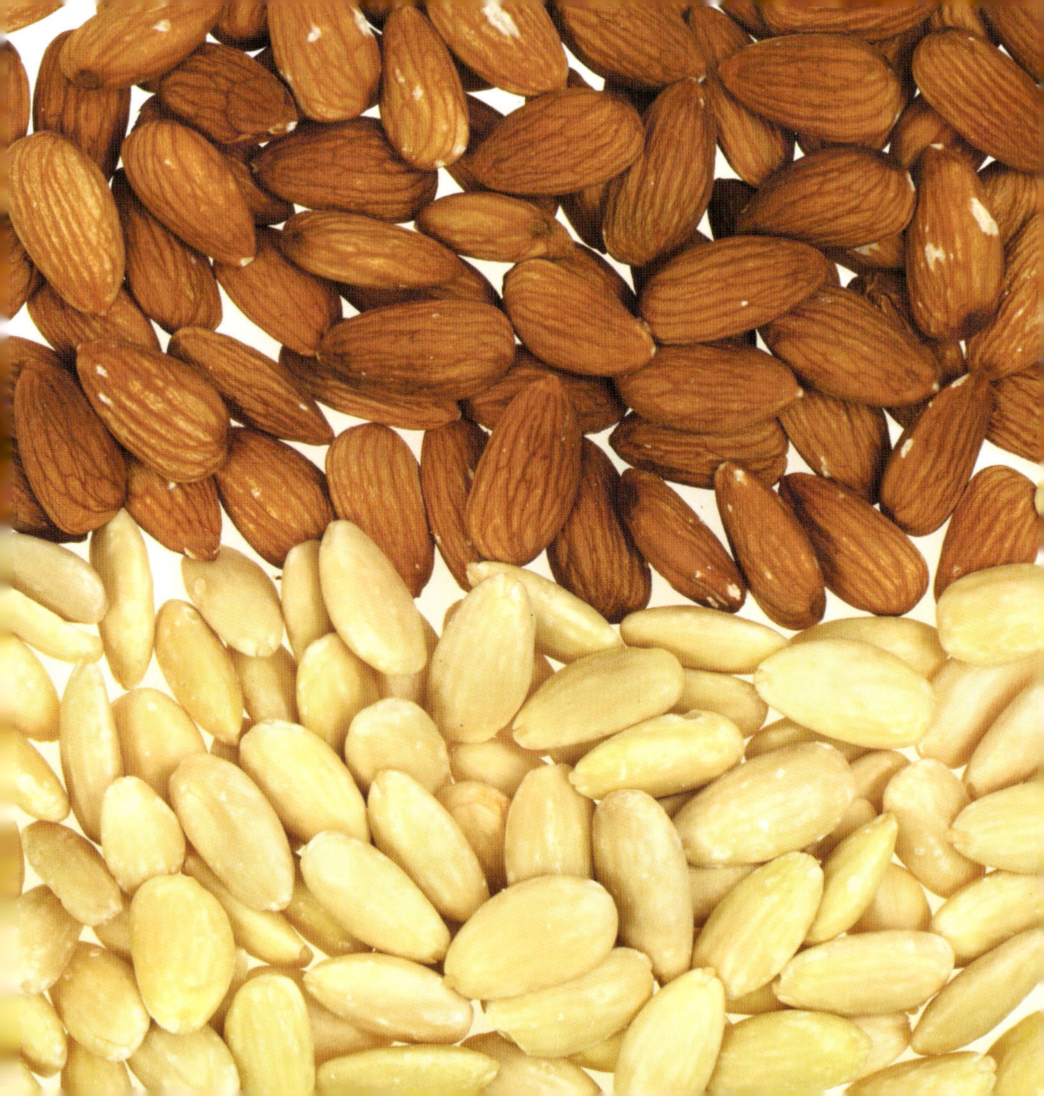

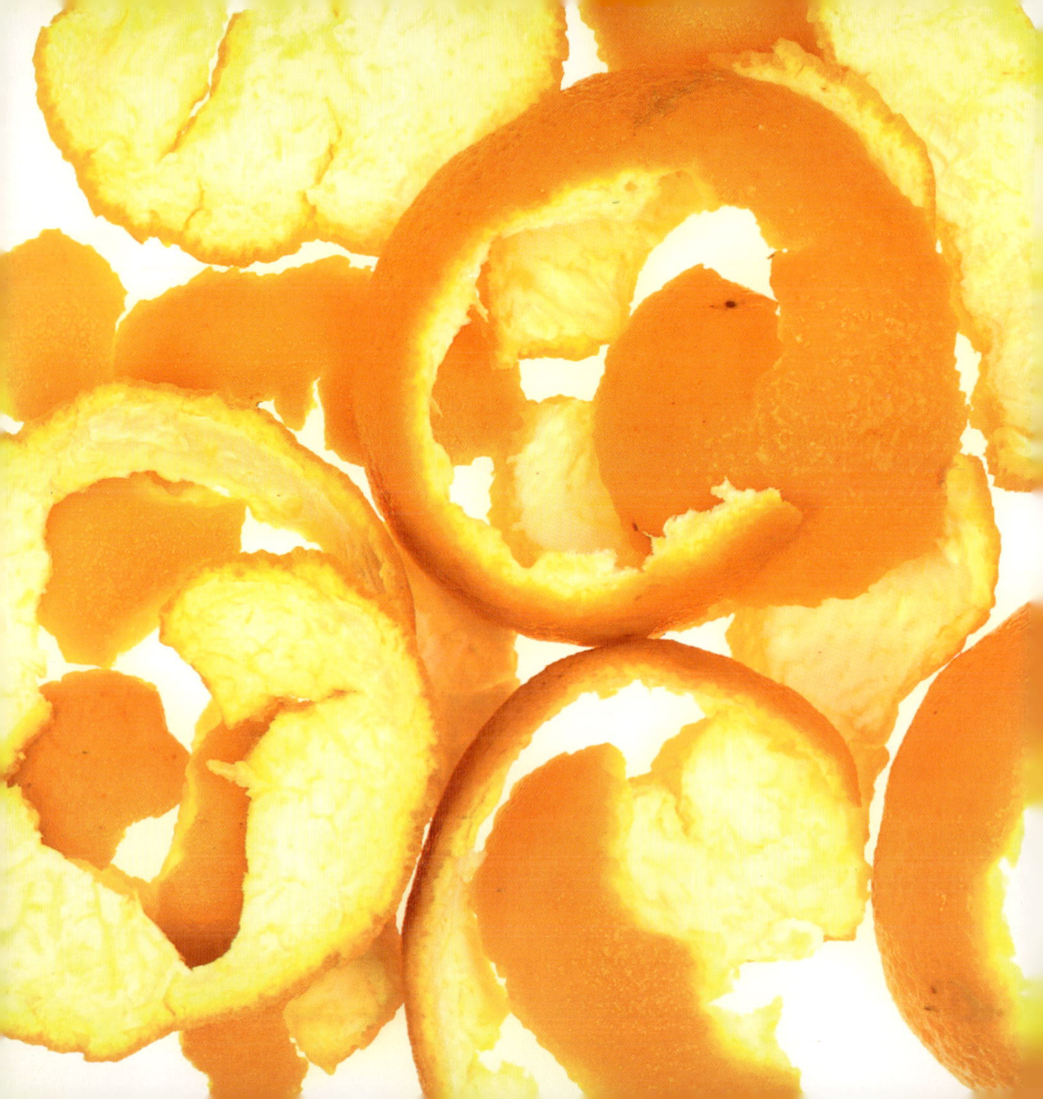

Citrus Reticulata

This is a deep orange oil expressed from tangerine peel that retains the scent of the fruit. In many ways it is similar to mandarin and sweet orange oils. It is good for skin problems including stretch marks and can help circulation in cold extremities, particularly the feet and hands. It helps the digestive system and can be beneficial in cases of constipation, diarrhea, and flatulence. It is another very good blender but be careful of its effect of increasing the skin's sensitivity to ultraviolet light.

Melaleuca Alternifolia

A colorless oil is produced from the leaves and twigs of the tea tree. It has a fresh, warm, and spicy fragrance. A highly antiseptic oil, it is very good for fungal infections including athlete's foot, candida, and ringworm. Acne, mouth ulcers, verrucae, cold sores, boils and spots, burns, sunburn, insect bites, and stings will all also benefit from this oil's properties. Certain respiratory conditions including bronchial and sinus congestion and sore throats can be helped too. Rather like lavender, tea tree is a very useful first aid oil and you will find it blends quite easily with other oils.

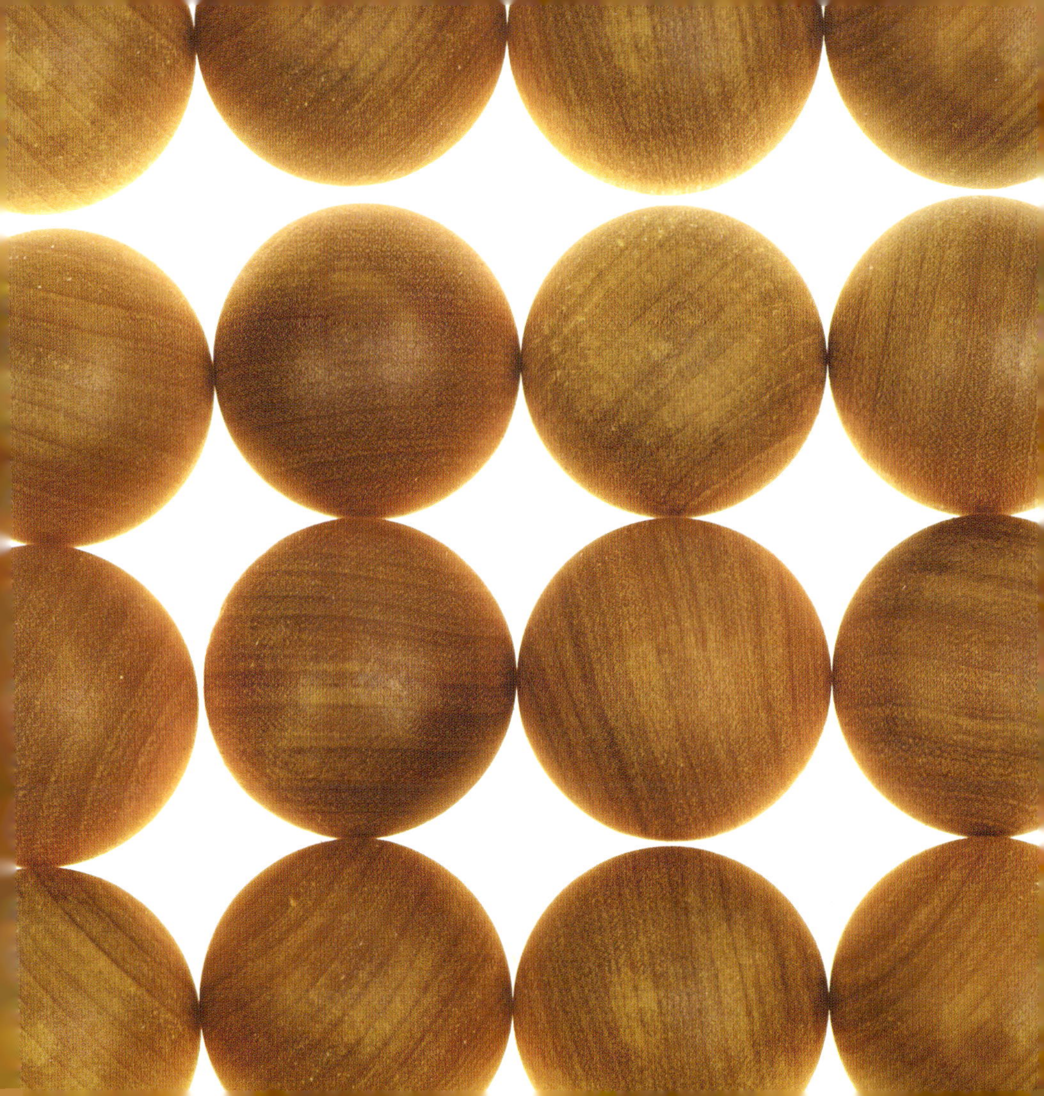

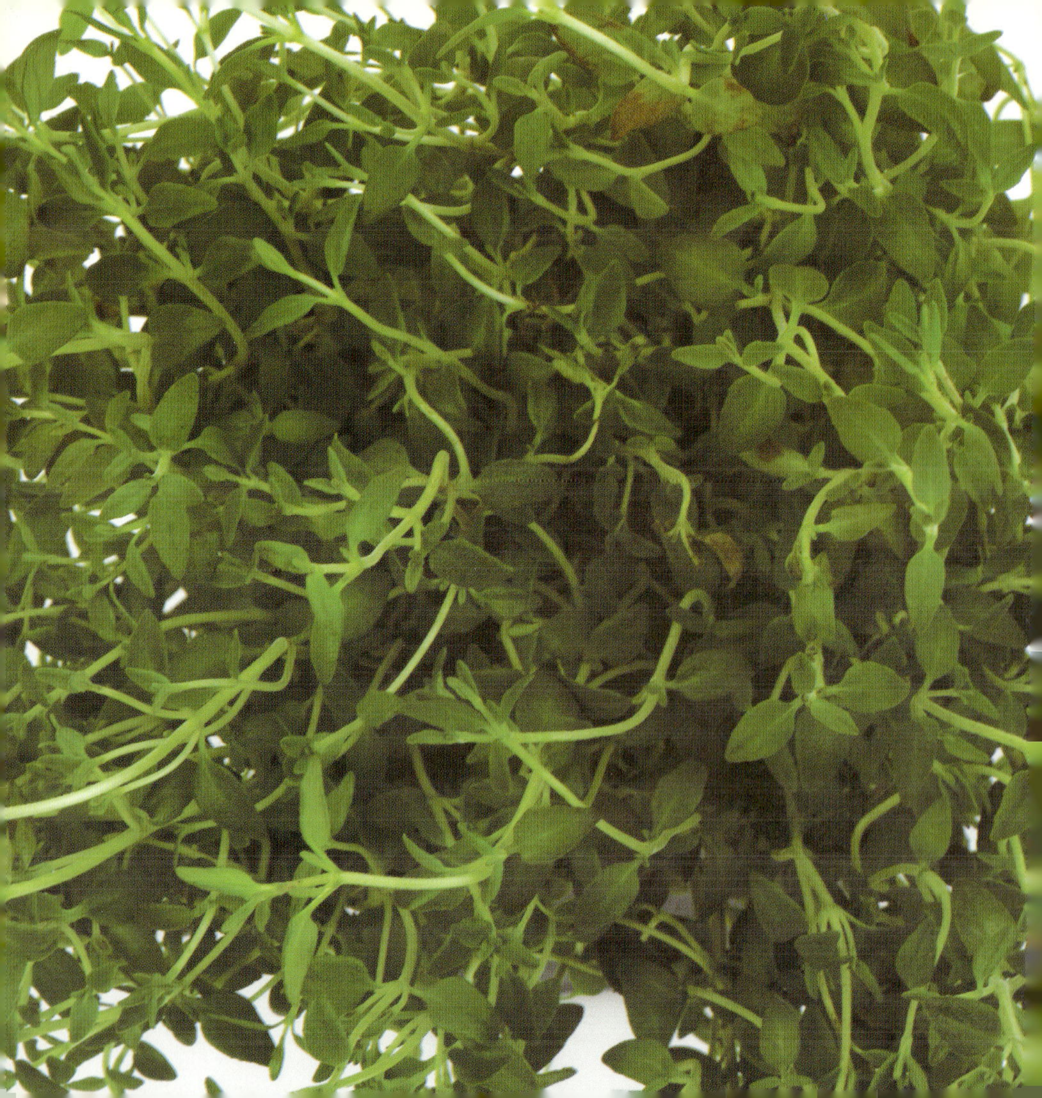

Thymus Vulgaris

A pale yellow oil with a spicy, herbaceous aroma. It is important that only white thyme oil is purchased. Extremely antiseptic and a general stimulant, particularly of capillary circulation, it makes a useful treatment for chilblains and cold extremities. Combined with diuretic properties it can be valuable for muscular aches and pains, gout, and arthritis. It can be used for respiratory problems including bronchitis, colds, influenza, and asthma. Once again it is a good insect repellent.

WARNING: Thyme should be avoided during pregnancy and may cause skin irritation in some people so use sparingly.

vetivert

Vetiveria Zizanoides

This is a greeny brown oil with a smoky, earthy fragrance. Known as "the oil of tranquillity" its name reflects its very calming effects, particularly on the central nervous system. It reduces tension and worry and also relieves anxiety and stress-related symptoms. Oily skin and acne may improve with vetivert oil, as may muscular aches and pains and rheumatism. It blends quite well with sandalwood, lavender, and ylang ylang. Commercially it is used as a fixative in the perfume industry.

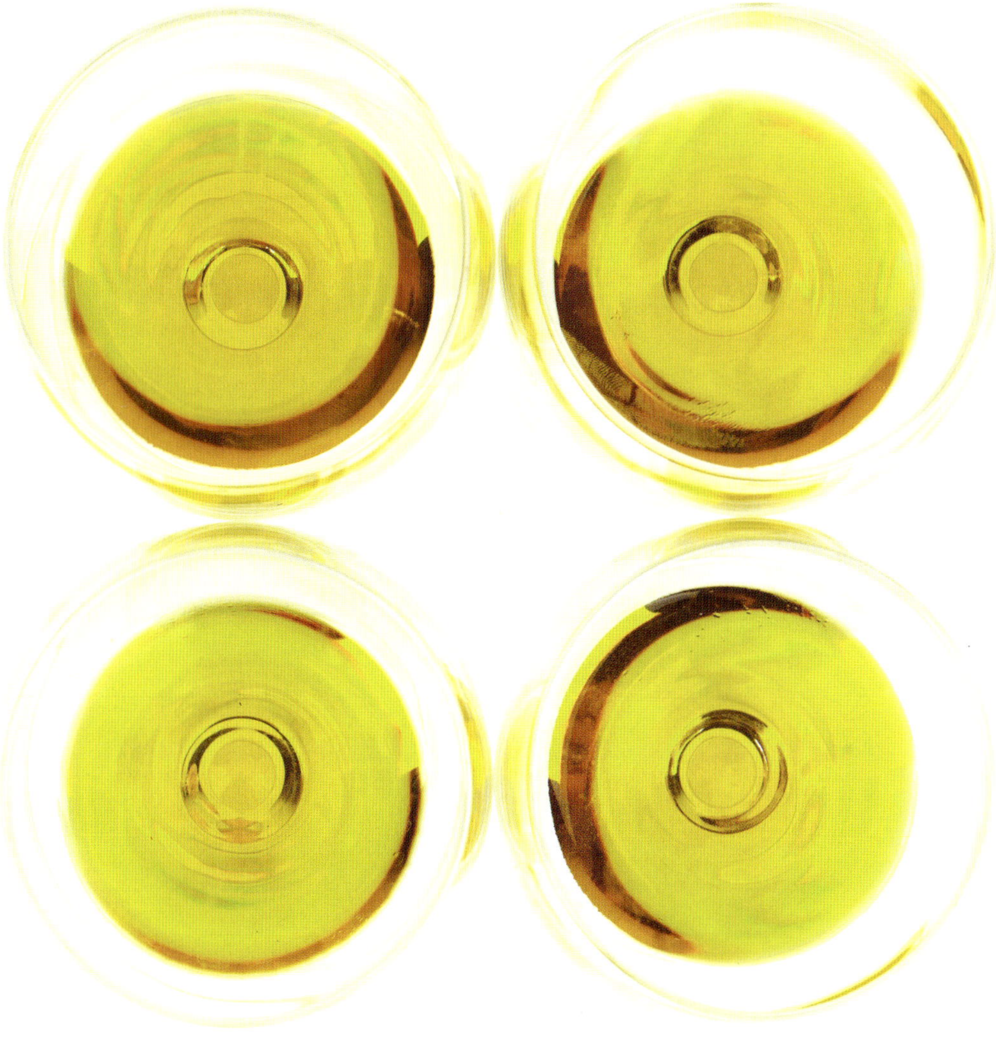

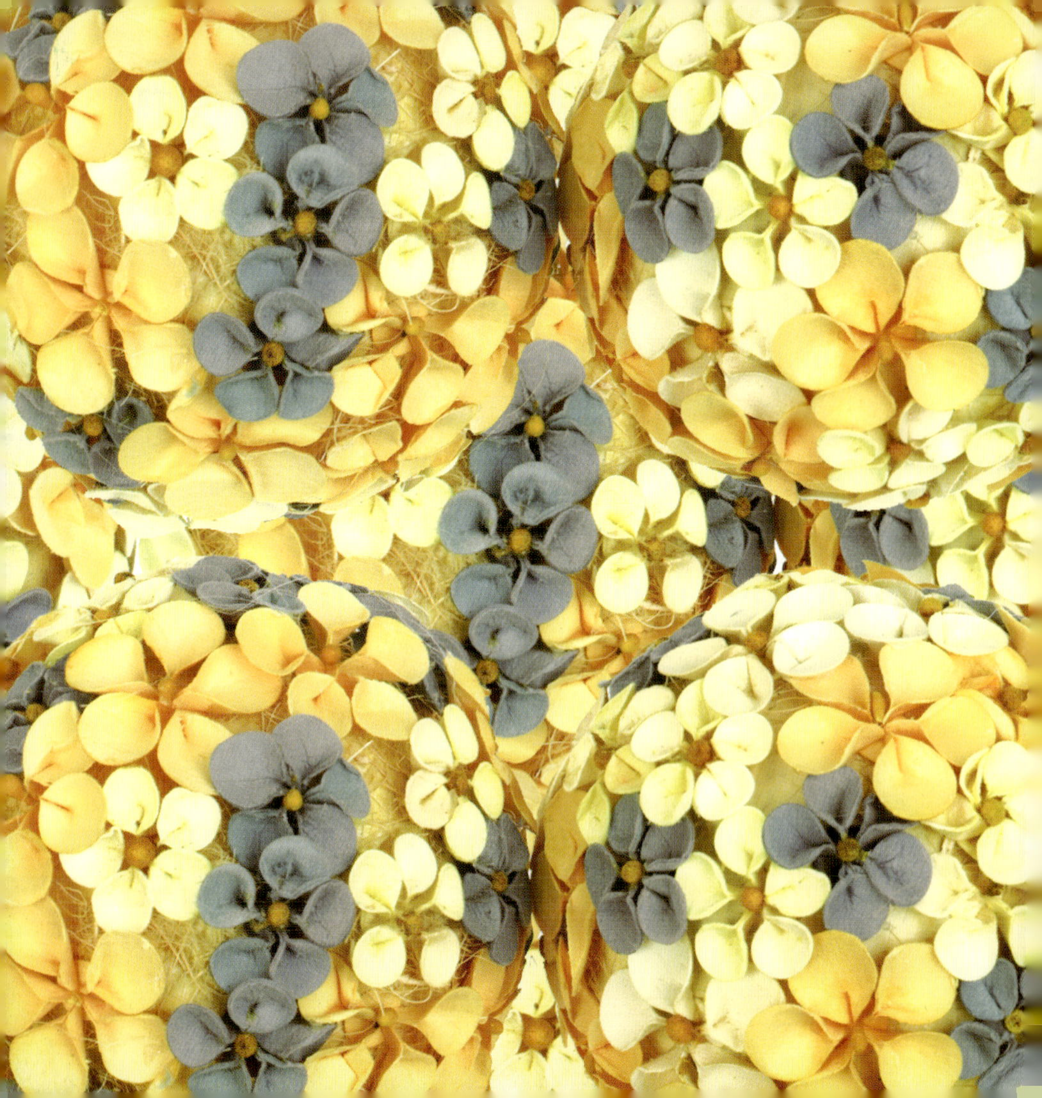

Cananga Odorata

This is a pale yellow oil with a very sweet, heady, floral aroma sometimes called "poor man's jasmine." It has a long reputation as an aphrodisiac and is recommended for impotence or frigidity. Sedative properties make it useful for anxiety and stress-related conditions as it slows the breathing and heart rates. Certain skin conditions, particularly acne or oily skin, can respond to this oil as it helps to balance sebum. However, beware, ylang ylang is a very powerful fragrance and should be used sparingly as too much can give you a headache. Try blending it with a light citrus oil.

closing

By now you should have some insight into the wonderful world of essential oils. Used carefully they can be amazingly beneficial but if in any doubt, please consult a reputable supplier or a qualified therapist.

Should you require further oils, make sure you obtain them from a reputable supplier.

WARNING: When burning the essential oils and incense cones contained in this pack, please ensure that the correct equipment is used. Never leave a burning item unattended.